AN ACCIDENTAL MOTHER

An
Accidental
Mother

Katherine Anne Kindred

UNBRIDLED BOOKS

Earlier versions of the essays "An Accidental Mother"
and "I Will Not Lie" were combined as one essay titled
"The Accidental Mother" and published in
the Spring 2008 issue of *Memoir (and)*.

Unbridled Books
Denver, Colorado

Drawings by Michael

Library of Congress Cataloging-in-Publication Data

Kindred, Katherine Anne.
An accidental mother / Katherine Anne Kindred.
p. cm.
ISBN 978-1-60953-058-7
1. Motherhood. 2. Parenting. 3. Separation
(Psychology)   I. Title.
HQ759.K543 2011
306.874'3—dc22
2011016104

1 3 5 7 9 10 8 6 4 2

Book Design by SH · CV

First Printing

Dedicated to the little boy who
gave me the greatest gift of all—motherhood.

Near or far, I will love you always.

An Accidental Mother

"Kate! There's a monster in my room!"

Still mostly asleep, I notice that without the help of my conscious mind to direct them, my legs have somehow begun on their own, swinging over the side of the bed, moving me toward the door of the room as my arms reach out in the dark for the small boy I know is somewhere near. I take his hand as my pupils begin to dilate enough to allow me to see down the hallway toward the glow of his bedroom nightlight.

"Let's go see," I whisper, and pull him gently along, reaching for the light switch the moment we pass through the doorway. The room is suddenly filled with light, and my eyes squint as I look around. I see an unmade bed with a Spiderman pillow in the middle, tiny jeans lying on the floor next to the laundry basket, storybooks on the table beside the bed.

"I don't see a monster," I say, and look down into the tear-filled eyes.

"It was in my dreams!" he tells me, and I notice he's been dragging his teddy bear along with him the whole time.

We're making progress, I think. For a long while he's been convinced that the monster is somewhere in his room. That he understands it's only in his dream is a giant step forward.

I pick him up to comfort him; he just turned five and is almost too big to hold, but he wraps his arms and legs around me and lays his head on my shoulder. I notice he is trembling. It only takes me a few minutes to get him snuggled back into bed, to reassure him that the monster dream is over, to tell him that instead he can dream about Grandma and Papa's house and going to the movies with his cousins.

I return to our bedroom and climb back into bed, now wide awake.

"Thanks for getting up with him," a voice whispers beside me.

"You're welcome," I whisper back.

That's when I realize the boy called out for me, not his dad, to protect him from the monster.

Me. Kate. Not his real mother, his accidental one.

I've never made any apologies for the fact that my only "child" turned out to be a border collie named Annie. I adopted her when she was two years old. Having come from an abusive home, she was skittish and needy. She's been with me for more than a decade, and I'm certain it's because of my patient nurturing that she now feels so well loved and secure that she disobeys nearly every command I offer—unless, of course, a biscuit is involved. She is smart and manipulative and I love her all the more for it. Yet she's well behaved enough that she travels with me everywhere and even comes to work with me every day.

We survived two failed relationships together, and after the second ended in divorce, I realized my opportunity to have children of the human kind had just passed me by. I accepted this fact without regret, content to consider Annie proof that *had I wanted to,* I could have raised a kind and loving child. Knowing my eggs weren't getting any younger, I opted for tubal ligation, certain that I could live a full life without experiencing the need to procreate or the pain of giving birth. This did not, however, mean I embraced a life of postdivorce solitude. Welcoming a barrage of blind dates, I soon learned that being childless at forty is a rarity. At my age nearly everyone single has at one point been married, and most of those marriages have resulted in a child or two. I joked to my girlfriends that surely I was meant to be a stepmother instead of a birth mother. Someday I would meet someone with two teenagers on their way to college who did not need a new mother and whose father was financially and emotionally prepared for a long-term casual commitment.

Obviously, I hadn't fully evaluated other possible outcomes.

Welcome Michael, just months shy of four years old, with dark-blond hair and big blue eyes, in dire need of a *mother.* Oh, and did I mention Jim, the ever handsome and charming father of said boy? The first time this child tested me with the word "mom" and then looked up into my eyes with a little grin, waiting, waiting, waiting to see what my response was going to be, I knew I was in deep trouble. His inquiries have continued, albeit with modifications along the way. Once I was paging through a magazine while he sat beside me with a coloring book and crayons, and he stopped to ask me if he had come out of my stomach.

"No," I told him, "you came out of your mother's stomach."

"But I want you to be my mother!"

I hesitated, then pulled out the bottom of my sweatshirt to make myself look pregnant. "Okay, get in my stomach."

Michael giggled. "Kate! You can't go backward!" And then, just as I begin to worry that the joke was improper, he asked, "What should I color next?"

As recommended by the family counselor, his father has provided Michael with a brief explanation, limited in detail. But it is nearly impossible to simplify such a complicated story.

Jim told me he received a phone call a little less than a year ago from a man who, unbeknownst to him, had been Michael's stepfather. Michael's mother, Jim's former girlfriend, was now married to another man— and addicted to prescription painkillers. She had been found unconscious in the backyard play-pool with Michael nearby. While she was hospitalized, state agencies intervened and mandated that she would not be allowed unsupervised contact with her child for the next two years.

Jim told me he had not known of the boy's existence and was shocked to learn he was father to a two-year-old son. Michael's mother relinquished all parental rights to Jim, and he flew five states away to begin parenting a child he had just met. To complicate things further, all of this occurred near the end of his marriage to the mother of his daughter, Elizabeth, Michael's half-sister.

Fast-forward one year, and into the picture steps Kate, with rose-colored glasses, obliterated fallopian tubes, and a sixty-pound border collie at her side.

After we were set up by a mutual friend, Jim was honest regarding his state of affairs during our long introductory telephone call. It was a complex history, for sure, but the fact that he had taken on the responsibility of raising his son alone, no questions asked, revealed his character. And failed relationships? How could I, twice divorced and also having experienced an unplanned pregnancy (that, although welcome at the time, ended in a miscarriage), judge him? My personal philosophy held that I would rather be guilty of ending a relationship than staying in a bad one for the sake of not being alone—or judged for what others might see as another failure. And so, while getting to know Jim, I kept an open mind.

After a week of telephone calls and a lunch date, I learned that we had a litany of common interests and an immediate attraction; we were soon inseparable. He seemed to be honest and ethical, was a committed father, and had a wit and sarcasm that challenged my own. To my surprise I was falling in love, even though this was a package deal. I was blissfully naive as to what that *really* meant.

As our relationship continued to develop, I tried to be as sensitive as possible to any long-term effects my presence might have on the children. Having given up on traditional commitment, I hadn't analyzed the consequences of this relationship lasting more than a few months. I was unprepared for how my role in Michael's life would become a primary one.

And then there was Elizabeth. I was careful to give her space and time to get to know me—she already had a mother. Yet every time she saw me she squealed with joy and wrapped her arms around my neck as I bent down to greet her. "Who's my chica?" I would ask. She always smiled and yelled out, "Me!"

I cautiously embraced these developing bonds, but before I recognized the potential demands, I became aware that my extracurricular interests required modifications. Dating a man with children meant that some nights there were no babysitters—no dining out, no dancing, no overnight Vegas turnarounds. Some nights the date consisted of macaroni and cheese, hot dogs, and a bedtime story after a bath. To some this might be cause to turn and run. But to my surprise, for me it became a toehold in a secret world, an exclusive club called "parenting," a world into which I had thought I would never be granted a pass. At the time, I didn't realize that it is also something like a cult—easier to get into than out of.

And therein lies the beauty of it—the tie that had never bound me before. The fact that Michael's mother is not present leaves me in a position where I cannot just break up, blame all the problems on the other person, and bail whenever I feel like it. That's no option when there is a little person in the other room waiting for me to tuck him in and read *Hop on Pop*. Furthermore, the sound of my voice as I rattle off a long list of complaints begins to sound a little ridiculous when I realize that the pile of dirty clothes on the floor is not nearly as scary as a monster hiding in a little boy's room three nights in a row.

Okay, so maybe I was supposed to learn something new about commitment. But I can't help but wonder if someone has made a mistake and why God, or the universe, or whoever is in charge, would allow me to become so involved in the development of this young boy. I am confident that I can screw up another relationship, but there are days when I am overwhelmed by the grave responsibility of the impact my words and actions have on this malleable little creature.

Before I met Jim and Michael, my job and my dog were my only priorities, with my social life coming in a close third. Managing the business interests of an entrepreneur consumed most of my time and energy, and knowing I could bring Annie to work made it easy for me to stay late into the evening and come to the office on the weekends. Although much of my job centered on accounting and management, the frequent event planning became an expression of my artistic talents. I relished the number of compliments handed out by important visitors and guests, not to mention my employer. Few would ever know how well I handled everything else, but a successfully executed extravaganza of a party for a hundred or more guests would be remembered for a long time. I happily accepted whatever credit was due, even though my role in planning a party was far less critical to my employer than how well I handled the bills and the banking.

I can't help but concede that the raising of a child can easily be compared to my job duties. No one will ever see all the effort a woman puts into making sure a child is "balanced," but everyone will notice how adorable the child looks if dressed up in designer clothes. And the part no one notices is much harder work.

There are days when I imagine simply running away, returning to a life in which my job, my boss, and my dog are my entire reason for being. Weeknights would mean dinner or a movie with friends, and my weekends would consist of at least one girl's night out. My excess cash would be spent on manicures and pedicures and the rare splurge on a pair of Jimmy Choos. But I have come to realize that as fond as I am of those days, I never fail to welcome the sight of the child standing before me, a miniature person with arms outstretched, begging me to hug him. So I have become an accidental mother to Michael. When he has a bad dream, he calls for me. When he can't get his pajama top off, I'm the one he comes to for help. When he is in need of snuggle time, mine is the first name from his lips.

During the first year of our relationship and after a change in his job schedule, Jim asked if I would help him get the kids to day care a few days a week.

Carrying my purse, my car keys, and a diaper bag, I would attempt to get Michael, Elizabeth, and Annie out the front door. Of course I carried my coffee cup, too, because I wouldn't be able to accomplish any of this without the help of a little caffeine. By the time I got everything and everybody out the front door, Annie had wandered into the farthest corner of the front yard to sniff around, Michael was distracted by whatever toy he had chosen to take to day care, and Elizabeth was looking at me, waiting for direction. I told them to come with me to the car as I opened all the doors, asking Michael to climb into his car seat while I picked up Elizabeth to hoist her into the back. After buckling Elizabeth in and walking around the car to secure Michael, I would spend half a minute coaxing Annie into the car. Continuing to sniff at first, pretending she couldn't hear me, she would suddenly lift her head and ears as though in surprise, dig in her back feet, and run past me to bolt up into the driver's seat. Once in the car, she would jump into the back-seat and turn around. I'd try to keep my coffee cup level with my left hand and throw my purse and the diaper bag into the front passenger seat with my right while Elizabeth and Michael complained about Annie's tail wagging in their faces. Yes, my beautiful sports car, the Jaguar I had proudly valet parked on so many Friday nights, was now overflowing with two kids in car seats and my dog squished in between them. Sliding into the front seat with a peek in the rearview mirror (and still trying not to spill my coffee), I'd swear my dog was smiling.

Helping them out of the car was easier, more so knowing they would soon be in more patient hands than mine. As I hugged Elizabeth good-bye, her little two-year-old body would squeeze me with a strength I could barely fathom; I bent down to kiss Michael, and he begged to know if I had lipstick on—already worried about a smudge on his cheek. I stood and shrugged in reply, but when I turned to walk away I found him wrapped around my legs within seconds. My heart filled in a way that was indescribable.

Another morning's routine was a similar struggle, minus Elizabeth because she was with her mother that week. Annie refused to get into the car, and Michael dropped his toys on the sidewalk because—surprise!— he wasn't paying attention.

As we drove to day care, Michael began to complain.

"Annie's paw is in my wap."

"*Lap,*" I said. "La la la la."

"La la la *lap*!"

"Try the word 'laughter.'"

"La la la *laughter*!" Then I heard a clatter in the backseat.

"I dropped my wed car!"

"Red, honey, it's *red.*"

"Wed."

"No, *rred.* Growl like a tiger . . . grrrrrrr!"

"Grrrrrrr!"

"Rrrrrrrrred!"

"*Rrrrrrrred!*" he yelled out.

I laughed at his exaggeration, but it didn't escape

me that I might have found a way to ensure that he didn't enter kindergarten with a speech impediment. For this, I was proud.

With my divorce came a resolute opposition to the traditional confines of marriage, yet I was hopeful that I would love again, was smart enough to never say never. Now the concept of marital ties pales in comparison with the responsibilities faced in becoming enmeshed in the lives of these children. The love for my man was just a small portion of the glue that bound me to what is beyond couple, to what begins to feel like family.

So I contemplated my history to date—boyfriends left behind, a failed cohabitation, two broken marriages, and my abandoned ovaries making certain I would never be required to have permanent ties to anyone. Unlike a birth mother, I would not be obligated by bloodlines and wouldn't have to worry about an abandoned child showing up on my doorstep demanding justification for my actions. Unlike a divorced mother, I would never be bound by legal documents or court orders that solidified an unbreakable connection to a man I no longer loved. I had the freedom to leave anytime.

Those days seem like a distant memory, and today Michael is a completely different child; no longer a toddler, he is now a *boy* and just starting first grade.

I am a different person as well. I no longer correct or attempt to explain when teachers or other mothers refer to me as "Michael's mom." Michael and I often look at each other and smile when this occurs, acknowledging what we feel for each other and sharing our little secret.

Now that we all live in the same house, the logistics of sharing in the responsibilities of the children's care are much easier. It is also a gift to start and end every single day with a kiss and a hug from a child I have come to love as though he were my own.

Although we have made the step to live together, Jim and I are both twice divorced and do not discuss marriage or the commingling of funds. Our bank accounts and other assets remain separate. But I do worry, with our bad track records, about what would happen to my relationship with Michael if mine with Jim were to falter. Jim's first divorce resulted in a severing of his relationship with a five-year-old stepdaughter, and a decade later I have seen him shed tears for that loss. Perhaps because of that heartbreak, he has promised that he will never keep Michael from me. In fact, I have asked Jim if I can adopt Michael, and he has agreed. But Jim is still in the middle of a drawn-out court battle with his ex-wife over custody of Elizabeth. Perhaps because the adoption requires more legal fees and another trip to court, he has not yet filed the required documentation. I know he's overwhelmed with the custody case, so I do not push. I have time, I think—it doesn't have to be done today. But I look forward to the legal affirmation of what I already feel.

It's been a short journey since those early months, when I worried about the extent of my role in Michael's life, wondered if I should hug him less or hug him more, asked myself if it was okay that he sometimes called me "Mom." Now I can hardly remember life without Michael, and entrusting his care to anyone else is unimaginable. His well-being is now my primary concern, and my entire life is planned around his school and activity schedule. My money is spent on his haircuts and school clothes; my evening priorities are homework and bath time. I am now privy to a host of previously undiscovered joys: the curiosity I often see in his big blue eyes; the beauty of his tiny freckles; the feel of his little hand snaking its way into mine; the preciousness of his tired body leaning against me.

Oftentimes I am in awe of the miracle of this boy, tearful at the privilege of being a part of his life. I cannot fathom how the one who gave birth to him could abandon him so completely, with nary a call or a letter in four years.

He did not come from my belly, and we have no genetic link, but he has become my sun, my moon, my stars. And I have become his mother.

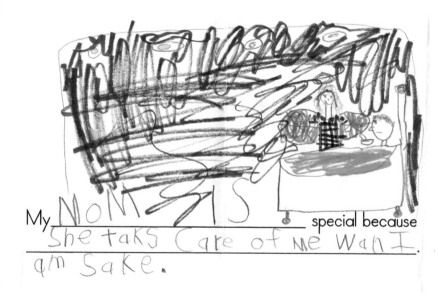

My NOM IS _____ special because
She taks Care of me Wan I
am Sake.

Michael Age Five, Elizabeth Age Three

Michael is standing next to Jim's horse, Cody, watching him roll the bit in his mouth. He turns to us and says, "Cody is getting old; his teeth are yellow and dirty. They look like Grandma's."

We are getting ready to run errands on a Saturday morning, and I ask Elizabeth if she will dress herself for me. She says no, but after a minute of thinking about it changes her mind and tells me yes. After what seems like a long time, I go upstairs to check on her. Elizabeth has on shorts and socks and is putting on her shoes—but she is wearing no shirt.

After I give Annie a bath and then dry her fur with the blow dryer, Michael says, "Kate! She looks brand-new!"

I'm driving Michael to day care, and we're listening to a music CD that I've been playing each morning for the last week. There is one particular song we both like, so I fast-forward to it. I sing along with the lyrics, and as the song nears its end and the final crescendo begins, Michael tell me, "Kate, this is the scary part!"

Jim decides to make the kids waffles for dinner. In one particular batch, he burns a few of the edges on one side. He transfers the waffles onto dinner plates, and I carry them to the table.

Michael pokes at his for a moment and then asks, "What's this black stuff for?"

I tell the children they need to take a nap, but they tell me they don't want to. Attempting to compromise, I say they can stay up for fifteen more minutes and then take their nap.

Elizabeth thinks about this and then asks, "How about five minutes?"

During a discussion with Michael over whether or not I should allow him to watch the television when he has such a poor attitude, he tells me, "I'd have a good attitude if I could watch cartoons."

It's the Saturday before Father's Day, and Jim is at work. Michael and I are rushing from store to store, running household errands and trying to gather gifts for his dad. By midafternoon we are both weary, and Michael is beginning to tune out everything I say. In addition, every time we pull into a parking space he asks me if he can bring his toys with us. Each time I repeat, "No, I've al-

ready told you that your toys can't come into the store."
When I ask him to get out of the car, he stalls by organiz-
ing the toys I have just told him cannot come with us. I
reach into the backseat, take the toys out of his hand and
place them on the opposite seat, then take his arm and
guide him out of the car. I am firm, and he is resisting.
Once out of the car I let go of his arm and then reach down
to hold his hand while we walk through the parking lot.

Instead of taking my hand, Michael looks up at me and
says, "You don't have to treat me like a bag!"

I own a charm bracelet with charms on every link repre-
senting things I've done or places I've been. Michael is
always telling me, "Kate! You should wear your bracelet
today!" He loves to look through the charms. On this day,
as we go through them together, he stops to examine a
heart charm. The charm opens and has slots on each side
for photos. I acquired it long before I knew Michael and
had meant to insert a picture of Annie.

"What is this charm for?" he queries.

"It's a place to put pictures of the people I love," I answer.

He tells me, "Well, you need a heart with three spaces, then: one for me, one for Daddy, and one for Elizabeth."

It is summer, another Saturday, and I'm doing dishes. Michael comes into the kitchen and stands next to me, and I turn to look his way. He is wearing shorts but no shirt and has put a small, round sticker on each of his nipples to cover them up.

This is my mother.

GOD

Today Michael asks me when he's going to see Boomer again. Boomer was Jim's dog who passed away last summer. I look around the room for help, but Jim is nowhere in sight. I'm on my own. I've come a long way since my Lutheran upbringing, and although I still don't have it all figured out, I am certain I don't believe in a singular Christian God or a literal heaven and hell. But Jim's family is Catholic, and Michael sometimes attends services with his grandparents. I decide it is best to respond accordingly and save my own, more complicated theories for when he is older.

"Boomer is in heaven with God."

"But I want to see Boomer now. How can I get to heaven?"

This is going to be a tough one. I think about the two baby ducks that died in our yard just weeks ago. A pair of adults landed in our backyard, hatched ten eggs, and swam around the pool with the babies for a week. By the end of the week most of the babies had disappeared, but we found two of them dead on the lawn. We were all in tears. I thought I recalled Jim telling the children that the babies had gone to heaven.

"We can't go to heaven until . . . we . . . die. Boomer died, so she's in heaven now, with the baby ducks."

"But if I die, I'll miss you!"

"You're not going to die for a long time. Not until you're old."

"How will I get to heaven?"

Even as an ex-Lutheran, these questions are way out of my league. But Michael, at five, just needs simple explanations.

"Your spirit will go to heaven, not your body."

"What's my spirit?"

Michael patiently awaits my response as it takes me a while to formulate an answer. "Well, you know how you have toys that have to run on a battery, and if the battery is dead the toy won't run?"

"Yes."

"Well, our spirit is sort of like the energy in a battery, and our body is the battery. The energy is what helps us walk and talk and love and laugh and cry and get mad and be ourselves. When our body gets old and run-down and worn-out, like an old battery, our spirit has to live somewhere else. So it goes to heaven to live with God. Heaven is a wonderful place. And when we go to heaven someday, we'll get to see Boomer again."

Michael's questions stop. He seems content with my answers, and I'm relieved. Then Jim appears, and I figure I'd better bring him up to speed. I have always done my best to respect his religious upbringing, but he knows I don't share his traditional beliefs.

"Michael and I were talking about Boomer, our spirit, and how when we die we go to heaven to be with God."

Jim begins to grin. "Oh, really? So you believe in God?"

Michael turns to me with his full attention. He is waiting.

"Well?" Jim asks.

I look down into the most beautiful eyes I've ever seen. "Of course I believe in God!"

Michael walks away, content, all of his questions having been answered.

Jim is now laughing.

If there is a God, he must have a really good sense of humor.

THE CURE FOR
A STOMACHACHE

We have just dropped off Michael's sister, returning her to her mother after a long weekend. Michael tells us he has a stomachache. I know Michael is not really sick. He's upset and probably doesn't even realize it.

When I was his age my father had a job in which he had to travel from time to time. Whenever he left home, I would go to my mother with an upset stomach. Sometimes I would ask for medicine, but my mother seemed to know that my pain was psychosomatic. Instead she would come home from the store with a book of paper dolls, and they would always distract me from thinking about my father's absence.

Now I look at Michael, and I'm certain his pain is emotional rather than physical. Perhaps he's upset that Elizabeth is leaving again. Perhaps he's upset because he senses that his father is upset.

Jim's ex-wife is attempting to gain full custody of Elizabeth. As far as I can see, Jim has done nothing to warrant losing his position as father. He is present, he is attentive, he is playful, he teaches his children the difference between right and wrong, he tells them he loves them. Of course I only know Jim's side of the story, but from what I can understand of the behavior I have witnessed, his ex-wife is not so much concerned about his parenting skills as just plain pissed off. The majority of her court filings reveal her belief that Jim is disrespecting her along with her concern that Jim will keep Elizabeth from her if he obtains custody—even though she's the one interfering with access. She believes he should retain no parental rights and seems focused on achieving that goal at any cost.

Having enjoyed a lengthy career in law enforcement, she is just a few years away from retiring, and to get caught committing perjury could threaten her certification. Although I am not with Jim during every interaction, I have been present during the majority of their exchanges and am privy to most of their correspondence. Therefore, I have firsthand knowledge that she has filed court documents containing lies, made false statements in order to obtain a protective injunction, and perjured herself in the courtroom. She has also called Jim's employer to file complaints against him and has reported to the city that our swimming pool has no fence.

Jim hires an attorney, and court documents are filed refuting her complaints. He fights the injunction in court, and it is overturned. His employer rejects her complaints as the unfounded attacks of a bitter ex-wife. The city inspector comes and sees that we have a motorized pool cover in compliance with city codes.

The injunction, although eventually dismissed, interferes with several weeks of Jim's parenting time, but Elizabeth's mother finds an abundance of other excuses to justify her failure to make the child available to her father. After moving forty miles away from Jim, she demands that he continue to pick up the child at day care in accordance with the court-ordered parenting plan—even though she has violated it herself by moving without prior notification and the required plan modification. Jim's work schedule and the long drive now make it impossible to pick up Elizabeth before day care closes.

Jim files pleadings to modify the parenting plan, and by the time the court date arrives he has missed several more weeks of parenting time. Elizabeth's mother suffers no consequences for violating the court orders, which is akin to dumping fuel on an open flame. Little do we know these are just the first in a long series of attacks.

These battles take their toll—on Jim, on me, on our relationship, and surely on the children. We don't discuss the court case or demean his ex-wife in front of either child, but no matter how much we try to mask our stress, the children sense it.

On this night we drop Elizabeth off, and I know Jim feels the strain of wondering whether his daughter will be delivered at the next scheduled time or whether his ex-wife will come up with a new method of interference. Although I am unsure whether Michael is upset because his sister has left again or because he senses his father's angst, what I do know is that I desperately want to stop Michael's pain.

On our way home we pull into a shopping plaza to pick up pool supplies, and I tell Jim I want to take Michael to the nearby department store. Michael holds my hand during the walk, and I ask if his stomach is feeling any better. He says it is not. I pretend I am there to shop for clothing, but I take him to the back of the store, where there is a very small toy department. I am hoping a new toy will distract him, as the paper dolls did me.

"Why don't you look around, pick something out?"

I am drawn to a row of stuffed animals—all soft, fluffy, adorable, and cuddly. Just looking at them makes *me* feel better. Michael is still young enough that he adores the stuffed animals he has at home. But I peer around the corner and see him holding a miniature treasure chest.

"Can I have this?" he asks.

I look at the tiny trunk and think that he will become bored with it quickly; once he hides something inside it, it will be cast aside.

"That's cool," I reply. I look around at the shelves near him and search for something I think will hold his interest for more than a few minutes. But the toy section is so small that there is little to choose from. I turn back to the stuffed animals. I grab a small but soft and floppy cat. I hold its head between my thumb and forefinger and its paws with my other hand. I step into the aisle, stretch it out toward Michael, and turn its head in his direction. It looks eerily real.

"Michael, I think this cat wants to come home with you." I turn the head further and wave at him with one of the cat's paws.

Michael smiles.

I make a little mewling sound and turn the head again. "I think he's talking to you."

Michael puts the treasure chest back on the shelf and reaches for the cat. He takes it out of my hands and pulls it close. "Can I have him?"

I nod in reply.

We go to the checkout, pay for the stuffed animal, and walk outside to meet Jim at the car. We all climb inside and buckle up.

"What'd you get?" Jim asks Michael.

"Show him," Michael says and hands me the cat.

I take the cat, holding its head and paws, and again turn the cat's head so that it is now looking toward Jim.

"It's Michael's new cat," I say, and then I wave at him with a paw. I'm surprised at how alive the little toy appears to be. I turn the head back toward Michael, and he reaches for it with tiny outstretched hands.

He holds the cat the entire way home.

Once back at the house, I get Michael ready for bed, helping him to brush his teeth and put on his pajamas. He climbs into bed holding the cat. "I want to sleep with him," he says. "Will you make it look real again?"

"Sure, honey." I tuck him in and then reach for the cat, turning the head to the side as though it is peering at Michael; then I bring it closer to kiss him on the cheek. He giggles and grabs the cat, pulling it under the covers with the head sticking out.

I lean in and kiss his forehead. "How's your stomach?" I ask.

"It's good."

"I'm glad it's feeling better. I love you, sweetie."

"I love you, too."

I get up and walk toward the door, reach for the light switch. "Good-night, Michael."

"Good-night, Kate."

"Good-night, Cat," I add.

Michael is suddenly pulling the cat out from under the covers. And then I see the tiny stuffed cat paw waving at me in reply.

The Tooth Fairy

I'm curled up in our bedroom chair reading a book when Jim enters the room. He says Michael has something important to tell me. Michael steps into the room with a grin, holding his hand out in front of him. In the center of his palm is a tiny tooth.

"You lost your first tooth! How exciting!" I'm out of the chair and walking over to hug him. "We have to call Grandma!"

"And Kiki, too!" he says, referring to my sister. "I'm going to put it under my pillow," he tells me, "and the tooth fairy is going to leave some money."

"How much do you think she'll leave?"

"A quarter . . . maybe a dollar." He pauses. "Maybe one hundred dollars!"

"Silly!" I say. "The tooth fairy doesn't leave *that* much money! Smile for me!"

He smiles, showing his teeth, and on the bottom row in the very front is a space so small I can hardly tell anything is missing.

"You look adorable! Let's go call Grandma!"

Michael's not a rough-and-tumble kind of boy, so I'm thrilled that losing his first tooth did not turn out to be traumatic. In fact, I'm surprised he's so calm about the whole thing.

As he makes his phone calls, I watch and listen. Although he is only in kindergarten, on the telephone he sounds as though he is completely grown up as he shares his story. Soon after the phone calls he is ready for bed and supervising Jim's placement of the tooth under his pillow.

.   .   .

The next morning Michael is already eating breakfast when I make my way to the kitchen.

"Did she come? Did she come?" I ask.

He smiles and nods.

"How much did she leave you?"

"A dollar!"

"A dollar? Oh, my gosh, that is so exciting! A dollar for your first tooth! Did you hear her?"

"No."

"I didn't hear anything either," I tell him.

"Neither did Daddy," he informs me. "But," and he pauses for effect, "I think I saw something sparkly!"

The School of
Repetition

When Michael first came into my life, he was almost three and a half and already potty trained. It wasn't until he started kindergarten that he began to get rather careless about wiping himself. It was only after gathering the laundry that I would realize the problem, yet repeated discussions were not making it go away. One afternoon as I was throwing laundry into the washing machine, I came across the most horrific display of failing to wipe I had seen yet. It was so bad that I put the underpants straight into a plastic bag and took them out to the Dumpster. I called Michael into the room, explained what I had found, and told him I was disgusted.

"You are more than old enough to remember to wipe yourself. If you are unable to do so, we may need to consider putting you into pull-ups."

"No!" he cried out, the thought as mortifying to him as what I had just witnessed in the laundry bin was to me.

I took him into the bathroom, closed the toilet lid, and asked him to sit down on top of it. "Now, I want you to tear off one tiny sheet of toilet paper and say out loud, 'When I poop, I wipe.'"

Michael wasn't happy but realized this was a lesser consequence than pull-ups. He tore off one square and said, "When I poop, I wipe."

"Good," I replied. "Now do it twenty-five times."

He opened his mouth to begin an argument, but I turned and walked away before he could say anything. Suddenly I worried that my response had been inappropriate. I listened from around the corner as he repeated the phrase over and over.

"Kate, I'm done," he eventually called out, and I walked in to retrieve the stack of tissues he now held in his hand.

"You have to remember to wipe yourself, Michael!"

"I know," he answered.

I don't know if a psychologist would approve of my methods, but there were no issues with Michael's laundry from that day forward.

My mother's name is __Kate__.

My mother is __29__ years old.

She always __is nice to me and buys me clothes and makes me dinner.__

I remember one time when __she made me a lot of ice crem. I like it when she does that.__

I usually call my mother
__Kate.__

I like to make her happy by __drawing things for her.__

The best thing about my mom is __shes always nice to me__

Michael Age Six, Elizabeth Age Four

....

Michael is supposed to be ready for school, but he hasn't come downstairs yet. I go up to check on him, and when I step into his bathroom he is holding his clothes in his hand, about to get dressed. When he sees me he is startled and tries to cover up his naked body with the loose clothing. In doing so, he steps backward and bumps his foot on a wooden stool.

"Ouch!" he yells.

"Honey, if you weren't trying so hard to cover yourself up, you wouldn't have hurt your foot. I've seen you without clothes since you were a little tiny boy!"

"Kate! That's different!" he replies.

"Why?" I query.

"Because! It was smaller then! It's bigger now!"

As we both climb into the car, Michael asks where we are going. I tell him we have numerous errands to run and places to go, including Target. After that we are stopping at Grandma's house for a visit.

Knowing Grandma's house is much more fun than running errands, Michael asks, "Why don't you take me to Grandma's house now and go to Target without me?"

We're driving in the car, and Elizabeth is looking at my sister's new tattoo. She says, "Kiki, I like your dragonflies."

Michael, not wanting to miss out on the conversation, chimes in, "Those are my favorite bugs."

I'm in Michael's bedroom, helping him pick out his clothes for school. I need to use the bathroom but don't want to go all the way back downstairs.

"Can I use your bathroom?" I ask.

Michael replies, "Yeah. I didn't poop, so it won't smell."

While chiding Jim over some minor sin, I tease him loudly: "You're fired!"

Michael steps over to me with concern on his face and says, "You can't fire him! I love him!" I'm looking down into his big blue eyes, trying to figure out how to reply, when he adds, "And you love him, too!"

It's Christmas Eve, and Grandma has called to talk to Michael. In addition to milk and cookies for Santa, she tells him he should leave out carrots for the reindeer. Once he has hung up the phone we head for the kitchen and begin to look through the refrigerator. I open up the vegetable drawer and see that we have no carrots.

"Now what do we do?" I ask.

"Why don't we leave them marshmallows?" he replies.

Elizabeth: "Daddy, where is the rain forest?"
Jim: "It's far, far away."
Elizabeth: "So if I ever go there, I better tinkle first."

It's a summer Saturday morning, and I'm sitting on the back patio reading a magazine and drinking my morning coffee. Michael is sitting in the chair next to me, playing a handheld electronic game. I get up and walk into the house, going into the kitchen to refill my coffee cup. Michael gets up and follows me, all the while with his eyes still on the game. I walk back out to the patio, and Michael follows me, still playing his game. Over the course of the next half hour, I get up two more times and return to the kitchen to refill my coffee, and each time Michael gets up with me, never saying a word and never looking up from his game. I'm not even sure he realizes he is following me.

One morning while walking to the bus stop, Michael asks me, "Kate, do you like having kids?"

My answer? "No, I love having kids."

Michael has two stuffed animals that are both becoming a little worse for wear. The stuffed dog's ear has fallen off, and the stuffed cat's nose has been partially chewed off by Jim's real dog, Max. I have just purchased a new sewing machine, and on this particular Saturday morning I set it up on the kitchen table and put the instructional video into the VCR.

About ten minutes into the video, Michael says, "Kate, while you're watching that video, think about the day you can sew my dog and my cat."

EXISTENCE

I am walking Michael to the bus stop when he turns to me and asks, "Kate, what if I wasn't made?"

"What do you mean?"

"What if no one built me?"

I ponder the question from a Catholic point of view, wondering how his father or grandmother would respond. I answer the question with another: "You mean what if God didn't make you?"

"Yeah."

"It would be awful! I would be so sad and so lonely!"

"You wouldn't have to be lonely; you'd be with Daddy."

"But I would still be lonely without you."

"But you wouldn't even know that I ever existed."

I am shocked that he has surmised this. But I stick to my message. "I would still miss you! I would just know that something wasn't right! And besides, who would I buy presents for?"

"Daddy. Or Gordon." Gordon is my boss.

"Gordon doesn't need presents; he can buy his own things. And besides, who would I take care of?"

"Gordon. And Daddy, too."

"But Michael," I say, "I can't read *Hop on Pop* to Gordon, now, can I?"

A big smile appears on his face, and he begins to giggle. Apparently the mental picture of me reading *Hop on Pop* to Gordon (who is a PhD) is just as humorous to Michael as it is to me. "Nooooo, I guess not."

As we reach the bus stop, his little hand firmly in mine, I wonder, how do these things come into a child's mind? What made him think of this? I look down at his beautiful little face, but before I can begin to question him, he speaks: "Kate, will you help me tie my shoe?"

As always, just as quickly as it has arrived, another moment of inquiry has passed.

I Will Not Lie

Along with all the joys, becoming a mother is hard work, requiring constant adjustments to address the needs and development of a child. Helping to enunciate *r*'s by growling like a tiger is far simpler than providing a moral compass. Case in point: try explaining to a child the importance of telling the truth when the truth may lead to punishment. When discussing the subject of lying with my adult friends, I have always given a stock response: "I never lie about anything important." This often-proffered sarcasm always raises a brow and brings on a bit of a laugh, but you cannot joke about such things to a child. To Michael I say that lying is a far worse offense than whatever thing he may have done to get into trouble and that he absolutely must tell the truth. He's only lied to us a handful of times (from what we can tell), but it seems that he always gets caught.

Now that Michael is of school age he is able to dress himself and pour his own bowl of cereal in the morning. He knows that after breakfast he is supposed to brush his teeth. He then ends up in my bathroom, where by this time I am dressed, made up, and finishing my hair, ready to help him comb his. Each day I ask him the same question: "Did you brush your teeth?"

On one such morning there is a slight pause before he says, "Yes." Something inside, perhaps the "mother truth detector," ticks, and I know he is lying.

"Are you sure?"

"Yes."

I lean in and look at him more closely, see dried

milk in the corners of his mouth. "You brushed your teeth?" I ask again.

"Yeeeesss!" he replies, obviously annoyed.

I look at his milk smile and am certain of the opposite. I march past him, up the stairs, through his bedroom, and into the bathroom, not looking back but knowing he is just a few feet behind me. I grab the electric toothbrush on the counter and run my finger over the bristles; they are dry. I open the bathroom drawer and (just to be sure) check his travel toothbrush, the one that goes with him on vacation or back and forth to Grandma's house. It, too, is stiff and unused. Of course I scold him, but there isn't time to do much about it—we're going to be late for the bus.

"We'll deal with this tonight," I say.

When Jim gets home I describe the morning's events. We sit Michael down together, and Jim tells him that although brushing his teeth is important, it is far more important to tell the truth. He explains that he is in trouble not for not brushing his teeth but for lying about it.

Jim pulls a notebook and a pencil out of a drawer and lays the notebook on the kitchen counter, scribbling across the top of the page.

"Can you read this?"

Michael nods and reads slowly, *"I will not lie."*

"Good. Now write it twenty-five times."

"What?" The boy is not happy.

"You better get started," Jim tells him and turns to walk away in a preemptive strike against the dirty look and slumped shoulders he knows will follow.

Later that night, long after Michael has been put to bed, I go into the kitchen to get a glass of water. I flip on the lights and see his scrawled lines. His printing is uneven, inconsistent, and slanting all over the page, just as you would expect from a six-year-old.

"I WILL NOT LIE."

His words yell out at me from the lined notebook paper, and I think, "How cute, how sad, how important," all at the same time. I realize that I wish Michael's behavior was perfect—not because I want him to be but because then we would never be required to discipline him.

A few days later I find myself arriving home long past Michael's bedtime after a lengthy work day, which included helping my boss to entertain a group of fifty business associates with an elaborate cocktail hour and dinner. I'm exhausted. Everyone is asleep, including the dog, and I can't wait to be. I've been on my feet running about all night, and all I want is to crawl into bed. And so I do.

The next morning Jim comes into the bedroom to say good-bye on his way to work. He declares that I must be sure to tell the boy that I went into his room and kissed him the night before because Michael told his dad to make certain I did.

I wander out to the kitchen in my robe and see Michael sitting at the counter, eating breakfast.

"Good morning, sunshine!" I call out.

He grins in return.

"Do you want to know what I did last night?" I ask.

He nods, still grinning.

"Well, I organized a party for a whole bunch of people. Then I wandered around and said hello to everyone and talked to them about business things. I made sure they all got dessert and then waited until everyone left to lock the doors and turn off the lights."

He knows me well enough that he attentively waits for the rest of the story.

"Then I came home, took off my shoes, tiptoed up the stairs, opened your bedroom door, and whispered, 'Michael, are you awake?'"

Now he's smiling.

"Do you know what I heard?"

He shakes his head.

I snort long and loud, imitating the snore I often hear from his father's side of the bed.

He starts to giggle. "Why didn't you wake me up?" he wants to know.

"I tried! I said, 'Michael, are you awake?' but all I heard was ..." and I begin the snorting again, even louder than before.

Now he's laughing out loud. "Kate!"

"It's true!" I say. "And then I leaned over to kiss you on the forehead. I whispered, 'Good-night, Michael—I hope you're having wonderful dreams.' And you know what I heard?"

Another smile, and an enthusiastic nod.

Snort, snort, ssnnoooorrrt—I fake-snore as loudly as I can.

He laughs again and returns to his breakfast. I pour my coffee. As I head back to the bedroom we both turn and smile at each other.

I never lie about anything important.

On this day, as I walk out of the kitchen, I can't imagine any lie as important as the one I've just told.

POLITICS 101

I used to be a Republican. Then I began to work for a very politically active Democrat. It was not he alone who converted me; it was what the Republicans did over the Monica Lewinsky incident. I'm not defending President Clinton's actions, and he shouldn't have lied, but I thought the reaction by the Republicans (and the amount of money their response cost taxpayers) was just as shameful. Even so, I was never motivated to change the designation on my voter registration until George W. Bush's second term.

My dog, Annie, came to the office with me daily.

Sometime during W's war against "terra," a visitor who knew that our office was filled with Democrats brought a plastic dog toy in Bush's likeness, although it was only his head and shoulders. My dog carried the toy around the office, and sometimes she chewed on it. But most of the time it remained upside down in her toy basket on the floor.

One Saturday afternoon Michael is playing with construction paper and crayons at the kitchen counter while I'm doing the dishes. He draws an American flag and then stops to look up at me.

"I want to draw things that are American. What else can I draw?"

"Hmmm, what about an eagle? An eagle is an American symbol."

"Okay!" He draws his version of a large bird. "What else?"

"Well, they say hot dogs and apple pie are American."

"How come?"

"I'm not sure why. But you could draw a hot dog, couldn't you?"

"Yes." A few minutes later a hot dog is drawn. It doesn't surprise me that he included ketchup in his drawing. He refuses to eat any meat without ketchup, but Jim and I decided long ago that it makes no difference to us if it ensures he'll finish his meal. "What else?" he inquires.

"What about the space shuttle or a spaceship? Americans made it to the moon before anyone else."

He's much more excited about drawing a rocket ship than he was about the hot dog. He bends his head, tongue curling up on his lip, concentrating quite hard on getting it right.

"Now what?"

I'm running out of ideas, and I have to think this over for a minute. "What about the president?"

"Oh! Good idea!" He starts to draw and then stops. Apparently drawing a president is harder than drawing a rocket or a hot dog. "I don't know how to draw his body." He pauses as he stops to think about it. "I know! I'll just draw his head—you know, like Annie's dog toy!"

LEFT OUT

Michael has been acting like a real pill lately, and after a couple of days of very un-Michael-like behavior, I sit down with him for a talk.

"What's going on with you?"

"I don't know."

"Are you feeling left out? Are you feeling sick? Are you tired?"

"I'm feeling left out."

Jim has warned me that children are near experts at acting like phony psychics—you have to be careful not to feed them answers. So I ask more questions. "Do you know what that means?"

He thinks about it for a very long time. "Well, it means you're not part of the family."

"That's crazy!" I say. I explain that he is the most important part of the family and that we love him more than anything. But it's true, I continue, that sometimes we forget to tell him because we get so busy with household chores, going to the grocery store, now Christmas shopping, and work. And we have to work so we can have money to buy food and clothes—and Christmas presents.

"Why can't just Daddy work?" he asks.

"Well, because if we both work, we can put all of our money together to buy the things we need as a family. And besides, part of my job is to take care of Gordon. And it's important to me to take care of Gordon, too."

He's quiet but seems somewhat satisfied with the conversation. After a long pause I begin to tickle him.

Then I read him a book, we snuggle, and I hug and kiss him.

He's been an angel ever since.

SOLITARY CONFINEMENT

It's Friday morning, and Jim has been out of town for the week, helping his father with the arrangements in preparation for his stepmother's memorial service. All of us, including the dogs, are out of sorts because of his absence.

One night Max wakes me at 11:30, jumping on the bed and sticking his nose in my face, something he never does. From that point on I am wide awake. Unable to go back to sleep, I turn the light on and read for an hour, then put the book down and try to doze off again.

At around 2:00 A.M. I hear Michael's footsteps clunking down the stairs, and he trudges into the bedroom, sniffling. "Kate, I had a bad dream!"

"What did you dream?"

"I dreamt that there was a talking mole!"

"A *what*?"

"A talking mole!"

I say nothing, trying to recall what a mole actually looks like.

"Will you please tuck me back into bed?"

We head upstairs, both dogs close at our heels. I send him to the bathroom, then try to remain patient while he reorganizes all the stuffed animals he sleeps with. Then I tuck him in, turn off the light, and return downstairs.

Now I am wide awake again. I decide to turn on the television. After about an hour I start to feel sleepy so I turn it off and finally drift back to sleep. The alarm rings way too early; I would give anything to stay in bed for another hour.

After a total of only five hours of sleep, most of it

interrupted, I'm a little cranky. I head upstairs to wake Michael, who is usually up by now. He is snoring loudly.

"Good morning, sunshine!" I call out.

The snoring stops, the eyes open, and he turns to look at me. I smile, then go into the closet to pick out his clothes for the day. "Get dressed for me, okay?"

"Kate, I'm *tired,*" he tells me.

"So am I."

"Why can't I sleep in?"

"Because you have school, silly. You can sleep in tomorrow."

We're running late today, and as usual I hear myself asking Michael to do the same things I ask him to do every morning. I can't fathom how, five months into the school year, he still can't remember what he is required to do each morning without instruction. But everyone assures me this is normal for a six-year-old.

"Go upstairs and brush your teeth."

"Don't forget to put your dirty clothes in the laundry basket."

"Did you turn your bedroom lights off?"

"Please put your shoes on."

Now he's in the bathroom with me as I finish my hair and makeup. We're arguing over the fact that he has failed to put on his sneakers, and after a long week alone and a night with no sleep, I'm becoming frustrated.

"Michael, why can't you remember? I tell you the same things every single solitary morning!"

He mumbles something under his breath, and I quickly assume he is about to sass me. I turn to him with the *you're in big trouble* look on my face.

"What did you just say?" I ask.

"Kate!" he exclaims. "I don't know what 'solitary' means!"

Michael Age Seven, Elizabeth Age Five

We're vacationing at Lake Powell, and Elizabeth is hiding behind the wall of our hotel-room patio, waiting for Jim to return from an errand so she can scare him. She turns to me and asks, "Should I say 'raaar' or 'boo'?"

We're getting ready to leave the house and trying to get the kids out to the garage and into the car. Jim tells Elizabeth to hurry.

Her reply? "I'll run like the weather!"

Although Michael usually eats his lunch in the school cafeteria, the fall camp requires that we pack a lunch for him. On this morning I drive all the way to school, and as we pull into the driveway to drop him off he announces that he has forgotten his lunch at home. I turn the car around and scold him, telling him that he needs to pay more attention; he's going to be late for camp and I'm going to be late for work. I believe my complaints are falling on deaf ears, but Michael suddenly interjects, "When Carson forgot his lunch, his mother didn't get mad at him."

Elizabeth is playing with her miniature Disney dolls and asks me to play, too. I pick up one of the tiny dolls and begin to talk in a silly voice, speaking for the little princess I'm holding. "'Hi! My name is Belle! My prince is named Jim, and he has two wonderful children named Michael and Elizabeth.'"

Elizabeth stops what she is doing, looks at me sternly, and says, "Kate! You have to pretend! It can't be real!"

I have an oversized chair in my bedroom, and I like to sit in it and read, my legs curled up beneath me, a blanket over my lap. The children know they can often find me in the chair on a Sunday afternoon and will often seek me out there, asking if I will come and get them a snack or put in a movie for them.

Michael's homework requires that he reads for a minimum of fifteen minutes each night. I find that if I read with him, he will be more inclined to do his assignment without complaining. Sometimes we read at the kitchen counter, sometimes at the kitchen table, and sometimes on the sofa.

One evening Michael asked me if we could read together in "the reading chair."

"Which chair is that?" I asked.

"The one in your bedroom."

It's my birthday, and as we walk to the bus stop, Michael asks, "Kate, how old are you?"

"Twenty-nine," I say.

"But you can't be twenty-nine; you were twenty-nine last year!"

"No, I'm really forty-six," I confess.

"That's old*!" he replies. After a few seconds of pondering, he asks, "How old is Daddy?"*

"He's forty-two."

"That can't be right!" he insists. "He's supposed to be older than you!"

It's Christmas morning, and Jim goes up to get the children to come down and open their gifts. Michael races down the stairs, around the Christmas tree, and right past the shiny new four-wheeled, kid-sized all-terrain vehicle parked beside it. He stops five feet past both and looks at the plate and glass that he left on the ledge in the living room the night before. He turns to us, points to the empty plate, and says, "Santa was here! The cookies are gone!"

Dear Mom,
I think that you are
the best Mom ever!
You're very loving and
nice. Thank you ▬
for helping me with
my homework every
night. I love you!

Rituals

Michael is reminding me of something I had forgotten from my childhood: rituals are important. As far as traditional rituals are concerned, I have always been a Scrooge of the worst kind. I hate Christmas shopping, haven't a clue how to cook a turkey, and refuse to acknowledge "Hallmark" holidays (those special days created by greeting-card companies to generate sales in between real holidays). But with Michael now a part of my life, Santa is back in action; Halloween costumes are an absolute necessity; and "Easter, the bunny," as Michael used to call him, has me boiling and coloring eggs and hiding them. What I am learning is that the big rituals are only a small part of what makes a childhood happy, secure, and special. Oftentimes those on a smaller scale seem to have the greatest impact. Unknowingly, I have created numerous rituals for Michael, completely unaware of the value he would place on them.

During dinner I always put ketchup on his plate in the shape of a giant smiley face.

After dinner, when he is settled into his bed, he asks, "Kate, what should I dream about?" Not answering the question is unacceptable; no matter how late it is or how far off the bedtime schedule we are, he will not go to sleep happily without an answer. He prefers the ones that are the most creative, and I always provide them with a very dramatic delivery.

"When you wake up in the morning ... you look out your window ... and find a roller coaster right outside the front door that will take you all the way to school!"

"When you get home from school tomorrow ...

you find a mountain in the backyard made of ice cream and chocolate syrup . . . with two giant spoons for you and Elizabeth!"

"When we come home from vacation . . . you find out that all of your stuffed animals have come to life!"

"When you walk into the backyard to throw the ball for Max . . . you see that the entire backyard has turned into a zoo . . . and there are elephants and giraffes and tigers and hippos all wandering around!"

In the morning there is a different routine: I step quietly into his room, walk over to the window to open the curtains, and then call out, "Good morning, sunshine!"

Michael has just started playing baseball, and I believe sports to be the best place to find rituals. He steps up to hit and taps his bat hard on home plate. In fact, I notice most of the boys doing it. Why are they tapping their bats on the plate? Surely they are mimicking older players; as far as I can see, there is no way a six-year-old could come up with a reason to tap the plate. As Michael gets up to bat, his team chants, "Let's go, Michael, *let's go!*" And once the game has ended? "Two, four, six, eight, who do we appreciate? *Cubs!*" Week after week, it is the same.

Interestingly, Michael has created many rituals himself. At six years old, he is still interested in stuffed animals, and I tend to come home from the mall with them sticking out of a purse or a pocket in order to surprise him. Years ago Michael slept with only his blue teddy bear, but as his collection has increased, things have become a little more complicated. As I watch him move the little creatures around the bed before I tuck him in, I wonder if his staging has a methodology or if the practice is simply meant to delay bedtime and prevent me from leaving the room. He still sleeps with Blue Bear, who goes on his right; the oversized stuffed dog that looks like a German shepherd is placed on his left. The majority of the toys are very small, and he lines them up alongside his pillow, some nights switching them from side to side. The last time I counted, he was keeping twenty-five stuffed animals in his bed, and each time he adds one to the mix it takes him longer to reorganize them before going to sleep. So is he just stalling, or is this a ritual that brings him comfort and consistency? Perhaps it is both.

Unknowingly, I am about to create a new ritual for us. It's the spring of 2006, and a new season of the hit television show *American Idol* is about to begin. The panel of judges (two record producers and a former pop-music star) have hit the road for the fifth year, visiting stadiums and concert halls across the country to give thousands of pop-star wannabes a one-song audition and the opportunity to compete for the title of the next "American Idol." Although the three judges select the group that will "go to Hollywood" (meaning the first major round of the competition), it is the American public who will ultimately select the next idol by phoning in votes for their favorites.

I saw only the end of the first season and missed those that followed. But the first-year winner, Kelly

Clarkson, had steady success, and eventually her second CD found its way into my car. I used to play it on the way to day care. Michael would tell me which songs were his favorites and ask me to play them over and over again. Kelly Clarkson walked away with a Grammy for that CD, and her renewed popularity reignited my interest in *Idol*. So when the fifth season was announced I decided to tune in.

One night after the first performer sang, Michael looked over to me and stuck his thumb sideways in the air. "Up or down?" he asked me.

Laughing aloud and certain he had learned this from someone at school, I immediately stuck my thumb up, confirming my approval of the performance. From then on, after every performance Michael would hold up his thumb and turn to me in question. When a contestant had an especially rough night, Michael and I would look at each other quickly, and I would watch the grin spread across his face as he followed my lead by giving the thumbs-down.

Every Tuesday after homework and dinner Michael

and I would settle down into the sofa while Jim walked past it, rolled his eyes, shook his head, and sneaked upstairs to hide out on his computer. Once Jim was out of the room Michael would smile at me and snuggle closer as we settled in to watch the evening unfold. Whether he really cared about any of these performers remains a mystery, but he seemed to treasure this shared time, having my full attention and engaging me in constant conversation, thrilled that I wanted his opinion about how someone sang or looked or whether they were going to get voted off.

As the weeks went by we were soon down to the last twenty contestants and found ourselves rooting for Elliott Yamin. He was small of stature, in need of orthodontics, and didn't have much stage presence, but his beautiful voice could send gooseflesh up and down my arms. To further justify our devotion, it was revealed that Elliott was not only struggling to manage diabetes but had a 90 percent hearing loss in one ear. The fact that he could carry a tune at all was extraordinary, let alone the fact that he was one of the best vocalists. Michael and I would always clap and cheer for Elliott, and from time to time, when his performance wasn't the best, we'd say, "Hang in there, Elliott!"

Soon the contenders were performing in a full concert hall with a much larger audience and a whole new set of pressures. We progressed from thumbs-up or -down to high-fiving, cheering, and whooping after each of Elliott's performances. Although I had instigated this game more for Michael's entertainment than my own, I had become attached to the idea of Elliott as the next American Idol. The first week his vote tally put him in the bottom, my heart sank. Later that night, alone in my bedroom and for the first time ever, I dialed the toll-free number to cast my vote for an *Idol* contestant. Initially my plan was never to admit it to anyone, not even on my deathbed. Any person who would sit around and watch a silly television show and then actually phone in votes must not have much of a life, I thought. But days later I sheepishly confessed to a friend that I had actually called in and placed a vote for Elliott. "Isn't that silly?" I asked.

"Are you kidding? Last week I voted for Chris, Catherine, and Elliott!" she told me.

That week the front page of the local newspaper reported that the show was averaging thirty-three million viewers each week and that on the previous night forty-five million votes had been cast. What was the population of the United States? I wondered. What percentage of our population was watching *American Idol*? And if there were 27 percent more votes than watchers, how many times were these people calling in? I didn't know if the thought that I was not alone in the mania comforted me or made me feel like I was just one of several million suckers.

We were into the final weeks, with only four players left and Elliott one of them. Michael and I clapped and cheered at Elliott's stellar performance. This close to the finale, the challengers were allowed two performances. As expected, everyone did well, but Elliott, the underdog, with nowhere to go but up, came alive. When his song was finished, the audience was on its feet. While I started clapping and cheering, Michael began to jump up and down on the sofa in joy. I turned to him and yelled, "Way to go, Elliott!" and lifted my hands to him for a high-ten. He slapped mine in return and kept jumping on the sofa (something that would not normally be allowed) as I jumped up and down on the floor.

At the end of the show I sent Michael upstairs to finish getting ready for bed. A few minutes later I stepped into his room to watch his organization of the stuffed animals into the hierarchy only he understands.

Pulling the blankets up to his chin, he asked, "Kate, what should I dream about?"

I thought for a moment and then began in my usual dramatic way, eyes wide open, speaking with long, drawn-out pauses.

"It's tomorrow night . . . we get home from your baseball game . . . we turn on the television . . . and we hear . . . the announcer . . . say, *'Elliott! You're through to the next round!'* "

"Kate! That's not a dream!"

"But it is! It's a good dream! Besides, we have to

root for Elliott so someday we can listen to his CD, just like we used to listen to Kelly Clarkson's! Did you know she was the first American Idol?"

Michael nodded regarding Kelly but had more questions about Elliott. "But Kate, why can't we just get his CD now?"

"Because he doesn't have one yet. And he'll only get to make one if he wins. So we have to keep rooting for him if we want him to be the next American Idol."

Michael stopped to think about this for a moment.

"Kate!" he suddenly exclaimed. "I have a better idea!"

"What is it, honey?" I asked; he had my full attention.

Michael began to mimic my dramatic storytelling style, with long pauses and intense eye contact. "To-morrow night . . . we'll go outside." He raised his little balled-up hand into the air and out popped one finger, pointing upward. "And then . . . we'll look . . . for . . . a wishing star!" He smiled grandly, obviously proud of his idea.

I am certain that at that particular moment, no real mom anywhere on the planet had a heart swelling with as much love as mine; no other mother loved her child as much as I loved this precious boy. This adorable creature—sweet, gentle, smart, thoughtful, and still smiling up at me, had become as much a son to me as any son could be. I tried to reply in the most cheerful tone, not wanting the tears welling in my eyes to be misunderstood. "Michael, that's the best idea ever!"

I tucked him in, leaving him surrounded by his stuffed animals, then slipped quietly downstairs to get myself ready for bed. Teeth brushed and my own "jammies" on, I made a detour on my way to the bed and grabbed the telephone. I confess, I voted for Elliott ten times.

I cast my votes for Elliott, but only some of them were for his singing. Most of them were simply cast in hope that a special ritual between a boy and his accidental mother could last for just a few more weeks.

THE MORE THE MERRIER

Both of us ready earlier than we need to be to get to the bus stop, I decide to fold some laundry at the kitchen table. Michael asks if he can play his Gameboy. I say yes, and he sits down at the table. I look at this cute little person sitting across from me and surprise myself with the words I hear coming from my lips: "I want more kids."

"You do?"

Not really, I think. Not the responsibility of it, not the worry of it, not the scariness of it. But the beauty of it, the bliss of it, being surrounded by adorable miniature persons who enrich your life on a daily basis. Little miracles, amazing creatures. And so I say, "Yeah, I want to have more."

"But you have Elizabeth, too."

"That's true."

"But we don't get to see her all the time," he says, his words echoing my thoughts.

"I know," I respond, certain we are both thinking that we wish she lived with us.

He continues, "Would you want a boy or a girl?"

"A boy!" I reply. "Then you'll have someone to play with!"

He thinks about this for a moment and then exclaims, "I know where we can get one!"

"You do?" I ask.

"Yeah! At the homeless place!"

Once I gather my wits, I tell him this is a great idea, and although I want to burst at the seams with laughter, I hold back my amusement. I tell him it's time to put on his jacket and get his backpack, filing our conversation into the "I must remember to tell his grandma" folder in my head.

I know that a while back his school class collected items to donate to a homeless shelter, yet it's unexpected that months later he would think of it, remain cognizant of the fact that some children are lacking in, or looking for, a home.

But I am even more surprised that Michael is not jealous or worried that another child might cause him to lose out on love, affection, or attention. I'm fairly certain his limited time with Elizabeth has helped him to realize that giving up anything you might be required to share is worth the gift that we call "family," the joy in being a part of something greater than ourselves.

And perhaps he is learning the same lesson that I have learned from becoming a part of this family: that sometimes more really is merrier.

Worry Has Its Rewards

I'm back on the couch. I could have stayed in bed, tried to silence Jim's snores with a pillow over my ears, but a handful of times each year his allergies become severe enough that it's impossible to quiet them even with goose down. The other reason I've left the bedroom is that, as usual, I've awakened to the point that my mind has begun to race and I am not the slightest bit sleepy, which means I must get up and read. I know that even if this were the quietest of nights, I would be unable to return to my dreams. Is it my age that makes getting a good night's sleep nearly impossible anymore, or is it the amount of responsibility I face? I'm in bed by 9:00 to watch the news, asleep by 10:00. But I awake sometime around 2:00 A.M. to toss and turn until an hour before the alarm is set to go off. I wonder whether, if I started going to bed at midnight, I could perhaps sleep until morning, but I know there's no way I could stay awake that late. The workday is only mildly tiring; it's my other vocation that has me worn out.

In the early months, when I was only "Daddy's girlfriend," it was easy to help when I wanted to and stand back when I didn't (or didn't know how). As our relationship grew into a serious, long-term commitment, I became a party to every aspect of parenting. I have learned that if one wishes to excel at it, there is not one detail that does not require the utmost in patience, discipline, consistency, and judgment. And I feel as though each day I fail in at least one of those areas, if not all of them.

To make matters more challenging, there is never a day off. Duty begins when I open the bedroom door and call out, "Good-morning, sunshine!" and pauses only once Michael is tucked into the middle of his bed and surrounded by his mountain of stuffed animals. Even when he's sound asleep, with snorts and snores that could compete with his father's in decibels, I know I am still on call.

He's older now and no longer has nighttime accidents. Nor does he get sick as often as he did when his immune system was constantly being tested in preschool. I can't recall the last time he had a nightmare, and it's been months since he sleepwalked. But the awareness that there is a young child sleeping in the room above mine who may require my care at any moment never ceases. The primary job of a parent seems to be worry.

I worry when he's asleep, I worry when he's at school, I worry when he's alone in his room. If he sleeps in on a Saturday, my first thought is that he's stopped breathing in the middle of the night. If he says his stomach is upset or he spends too much time in the bathroom, I worry that his digestive system might be malfunctioning. When I hug him good-bye and he feels hot, I wonder if he might be getting another ear infection. And I then try to recall where I heard that a low-grade fever is symptomatic of childhood leukemia. Frustrated because he won't look both ways when crossing the street on the way to the bus stop, I tell him about my girlfriend in the third grade who got hit by a car in the crosswalk, went flying through the air, and had her leg severely broken. When he replies, "She was flying? Cool!" I decide I will not allow him to cross a street without me until he's sixteen. Is he skinny because he's a typical growing grade schooler who hates vegetables, or are we guilty of poor parenting because his breakfast consists of Froot Loops instead of fruit?

And his physical safety is only a very small part of my obsession because far worse than the thought that he may get sick or hurt on my watch is the fact that his father and I are inevitably going to screw up his psyche.

Jim and I have weathered many challenges in our relationship, but it is hard to hide tension and upset from a child. As the years have rolled along and Elizabeth's custody fight has progressed, it seems the time and energy we might have used to work on our own issues has been given to Jim's ex-wife. I have come to realize that that relationship has remained more primary than the one he shares with me. So now I worry that we're not showing Michael the best example of what a good, healthy, committed relationship should look like.

I want to work on our issues, and I don't want the custody war to define our life together. Jim has agreed to see the family counselor, but for me, new hurdles have arisen. The accusatory court filings and psychiatric custody evaluations have raised questions about Jim's role in his previous relationships and of course caused anxiety for me over our future together. A fight is never one-sided, and as much as Jim appears to be the victim, I know there must be more that I do not know. Why is his ex-wife so vengeful? Why does she want to hurt him so? Why is she fearful that he would keep Elizabeth from her?

And then there is Michael's mother. After receiving the final custody evaluation, Jim learned that his ex-wife had Michael's mother interviewed by phone for the evaluation—without Jim's knowledge or participation, as is required by the rules. Although the written report claims that Michael's mother expressed no issues with Jim's parenting abilities, she told the evaluator that Jim had known about her pregnancy. Jim swore to me that Michael's mother said she was pregnant the same day he told her he wanted out of the relationship; he was convinced she was lying in a ploy to prevent him from breaking up with her. His explanations only leave me more confused.

With her contact information now in hand, Jim telephoned Michael's mother. After a lengthy phone call discussing the best way to reopen dialogue between mother and son, she promised to call back at a scheduled time to talk to Michael. Sadly, she did not call at the scheduled time, or ever again. At least not to my knowledge.

Because we struggle with our finances, I asked Jim why he couldn't seek child support from Michael's mother. He replied that he would never do that because he didn't want to encourage her to have contact with Michael. He claimed he had no way to know the status of her drug addiction. Further, he stated that her failure to contact Michael in the years since her overdose and her obvious lack of dependability would only cause more confusion for the boy. But I worry that his complete lack of a relationship with his real mother will cause Michael other problems.

Jim has told Michael only that his mother is sick and cannot take care of him, but as Michael gets older that explanation will require more details and surely bring about more questions. It's true, she lives far away and at best could achieve only limited contact. But as Jim insists that his ex-wife has no right to interfere in his relationship with Elizabeth, he justifies his own control over Michael's relationship with his mother. I also wonder if it is that desire for control that has caused Jim to put off filing the court documents—as he had agreed to do—to allow me to adopt Michael.

But what if Michael's mother is no longer on drugs? What if she is remorseful? As much as I may fill the role of mother for Michael, should he not somehow have a chance to know his real one—for good or bad?

It is these bigger issues that cause my greatest worries.

Still, I struggle with the day-to-day ordinary ways in which I fear I will screw up the child. When I hear him telling his sister that he can't play a certain game with her because he's "too busy," I realize that I have been telling him the same thing all weekend long while cleaning house and doing laundry. When he uncharacteristically punches the sofa when he isn't getting his way, I question whether it is because he's cranky and tired from staying up too late the night before or whether we have inadvertently turned him toward a life of violence because he received a spanking when he was four. I wonder what he will remember most as an adult—the red ketchup smiley faces I drew on his plate or the red time-out chair?

From time to time I voice these concerns with the other moms at the bus stop, who, although younger, are more experienced than I because they all have multiple children, most of whom are older than Michael.

"It takes him forever to get ready in the morning," I say. "He can't remember the simplest of tasks."

"Boys are always getting distracted; it's normal that they are unable to remember what you just told them to do," one mother tells me. "Starting a chore chart on a chalkboard might help. If they do their chores, they get an allowance. Then you divide the allowance into one of three jars: one for spending, one for saving, and one for charity."

When Michael was four we had a chore chart with smiley-face stickers. It had such grave responsibilities as putting away his toys and taking his dinner plate to the counter. He got an allowance for it, but none of us (including Michael) remembered to follow it on a daily basis, and somehow it fell by the wayside. I want him to learn about money and responsibilities, give him a start at learning good fiscal habits at a young age, and I want to help him understand the importance of saving before spending. But I didn't know I was supposed to have *jars*. And now I have dropped the ball in teaching him about not only money but the importance of charity.

To add to my guilt, I am the only mother at the bus stop who is required to work, meaning Michael is the only child who has to go to after-school care. The other moms spend their days taking yoga and spin classes before going to volunteer at the school; they pick their kids up when class is over and cart their multiple children around to swim meets and sporting events. I signed Michael up for keyboard classes and golf partly because they meet on the school grounds after classes let out—no carting around required. In the summers these same mothers take their children to the beach for a month-long vacation while Michael is stuck in day care three, sometimes four days a week. What on earth do these neighborhood fathers do for a living to be able to afford two and three children, a stay-at-home wife, grade school sports, and a summer rental? I make a generous salary with beyond-normal benefits, yet combined with Jim's wage as a police officer, we shop for our clothes on sale racks and have yet to start a college fund.

When I get home from work at 5:00, we figure out what we're eating, throw in a load of laundry, and then feed the dogs while Michael pulls his homework folder out of his backpack. Michael is tired and distracted, but his schoolwork requires that we become teachers from 5:00 to 6:00. His homework can't be completed without help, and he is required to read and play his keyboard every day. So his homework becomes our homework. One night I decide to cheat and read the word for him because he can't make it out; his father, in the kitchen with us beginning dinner preparations, interjects in a whisper that I need to let him figure it out on his own.

"But the word is *sorcerer*," I explain. "We'll be here all night."

And now I fail the job of teacher.

Michael's real teacher sends a note that he needs to bring apples to school the next day. They must be different colors, and we must tell him what kind they are. So either prior to eating dinner or after it, one of us must drive to the market so that Michael can do "his" homework. By the time Michael is in bed (after having been reminded to brush his teeth and go potty and close his drawers and turn off his lights and pick up his dirty clothes and put away his toys), we are all worn-out.

Sometime after 8:30, I get to begin "my time." Time to write, time to quilt, time to do crafts, time to journal, time to read. (Relationship time is out of the question, as Jim is checking his e-mail and washing his uniforms, planning on going to bed early so that he may be well rested for his ten-hour workday.) I should write, I should sew, I should draw, yet all I want to do is sleep. I brush my teeth, wash my face, put on my pajamas, and turn on the television. By 9:00 I can hardly keep my eyes open and inevitably drift off in the middle of the nightly news.

Yes, I worry about everything, and perhaps it seems as though I am complaining, but I really don't mean it to be a complaint. The fact is—with all my heart—I love Michael, and I love his father, and I love the role of mother. I love how Michael grins when I say, "Good morning, sunshine!" I love how he hugs me good-bye, and I love to listen to him read to me. I am thrilled when he asks me questions about the world that I actually have the answers to, and I love that when we are all out together, it is my hand Michael prefers to hold.

I love, too, that I have been the primary woman in Michael's life and that I am witness to my influence. His grandmother tells me how much he mimics me when he is in her care. "Grandma, I'm *serious*!" he says, the "I'm serious" a phrase I use often in his presence.

"Grandma, we could always order *in* for dinner," he tells her when she wonders what to cook. My lessons for him come back to me daily. "Get dressed, Michael." I say, and he corrects me: "You mean *please* get dressed."

Parenting is a hard job, but it is filled with the best of rewards. I give, and I get so much more in return. But I do worry that somehow I will fail Michael in every way possible.

Another night I awake at 2:00 in the morning. Tonight there is no snoring, but I am still wide awake, thinking about our day. I put chocolate chips in Michael's ice cream tonight, and you would have thought it was the best thing to ever happen to him. But we only read for ten minutes when we were supposed to read for fifteen, and I forgot to have him practice writing his letters. Will his ability to read and write be stunted? Will he blame me if he has trouble in junior high? I know it is likely there will come a time in his life when he will spend a portion of his adulthood focusing on all we've done wrong. But I wonder, will he remember only that, or will he also recall the chocolate chips in his ice cream?

I travel to Aspen for a week to attend a writer's conference, and Michael and his father drop me off at the airport curb with kisses and hugs. Before I even make it to the check-in kiosk, my cell phone is ringing. My phone is too difficult to get to as I am checking my bag and getting my boarding pass, so when I'm finished I walk around a hidden corner to return the call.

The only thing I can hear on the other end of the line is the sound of a little boy sobbing. There are no words because he cannot get them out.

"It's okay, honey," I say, "I'll be back in a few days, I promise."

I turn into the wall, not wanting anyone to see the tears now streaming down my face. I choke on my words, try to hide that I'm upset, too.

"I love you very much, honey," I whisper.

He still says nothing, his cries unabated.

"I promise, the time will go by so fast, I'll be back before you know it."

He's still crying, but now not quite as hard.

"Are you going to be okay?"

He still doesn't answer.

I wait in silence, not sure what to say to comfort him.

"I love you," I say again.

He gives the phone back to Daddy, who tells me the worst of it seems to have passed. We say our good-byes, and I gather my belongings to make the trek to the gate, wiping the last tear from my cheek.

I realize that with all my worrying, I must be doing something right. What could be further proof than the tears of a boy over the absence of his mother?

Michael Age Eight, Elizabeth Age Six

Elizabeth has watched American Idol *at her mother's house, and she knows Michael and I have been fans of Elliott Yamin. During the period in which Kelly Clarkson played in my car stereo on the way to day care, Elizabeth was often with us. Jim liked to tease us about watching* American Idol, *and the three of us always defended our favorites.*

On this particular Friday night I get home from work, and Michael and Elizabeth come running to greet me.

"Where's Daddy?" I ask.

"He's taking a nap," Elizabeth says. "And Kate, Daddy called you Kate Schmate!"

Michael then tells me, "And he called Elliott, Elliott Schmelliott!"

Elizabeth adds, "He called Kelly Clarkson something, too!"

Michael is petting our dog Max, who has bad breath. "Today is the happiest day of my life," he tells me.

"Why?" I ask.

"Because Max is getting his teeth cleaned."

Elizabeth tells Jim, "I have a song that I keep hearing in my head over and over again, and I can't get it to stop!" Then she pauses. "Oh, wait—it stopped!" Then another pause. "Oh—it started again!"

I'm picking up Michael from a pool party on the afternoon of his last day of school, and he tells me, "Kate, I don't want second grade to be over."

We're getting into the pool, and Michael asks Elizabeth, "Have you ever heard of the Titanic?"

Elizabeth tells him no.

Michael says, "It was this big cruise ship that hit an icebox, and all the rich people who were on the top of the boat got into the life rafts and survived, but all the poor people sunk!"

Elizabeth asks, "And then what happened to them?"

Michael thinks about this for a few seconds. "Well, they drowned."

"You mean they died?"

"Yeah," Michael replies.

"Oh."

And the conversation is unexpectedly over, and they are on to the next one.

Somewhere along the line I created a game of playing "beauty shop" with Elizabeth in order to keep her atten-

tion long enough to comb out and style her long hair. When I pretend to be "Rebecca," the beauty-shop owner, I find that Elizabeth is much more patient about letting me comb out her tangles. Elizabeth adores playing pretend, so it seems that each time I ask if we can fix her hair, she says, "Kate, will you play Rebecca?" I oblige her, and Elizabeth pretends she is Sleeping Beauty. I talk to her as though she is a real client, asking her what's new and how her week has been, and I pretend to write down future appointments with an imaginary pencil on my bathroom countertop. One afternoon we all climb into the car to run errands, and Elizabeth is telling Daddy about her trip to "Rebecca's beauty shop."

Suddenly Michael pipes up, "Kate, you look a lot like Rebecca."

My mom is funny because she calls me funny names.

I love my mom because she cleans my room, buys toys for me, and how she makes tacos for me.

My mom makes great tacos, she only puts the stuff I like inside the taco. They taste so good.

My mom always wants everything to be neat and in its place. And when she cleans my room, thats exactly how she does it!

My mom buys the toys I want, such as Pokemon cards. But sometimes she wants me to use my own money. But I think it's unfare. I don't kow why.

I love my mom so much! have a happy mothers day, mom!

A Bad Employee

This morning, as eight-year-old Michael stood before the bathroom mirror making faces, I reminded him for what felt like the thousandth time that he was supposed to be brushing his teeth. We had only five minutes before we had to leave to make it to the bus stop on time, and we still had to put on his shoes, pick out a snack, gather his homework, and prepare his backpack. I remained calm, but I asked myself, Why is this so difficult? Why can't he just do what he knows he's supposed to do? And if he can't, why can't I be more understanding? After all, who wouldn't rather make faces in the mirror than have to brush one's teeth?

And then it hit me. Having an eight-year-old is like having an insubordinate employee. We've all had experiences either as a manager or a coworker in dealing with a fellow employee who consistently fails to adequately perform the requirements of the job.

These are the traits I would use to describe a bad employee:

- Is easily distracted; can't focus on the job
- Has to be told repeatedly what to do
- Is argumentative
- Is frequently tardy
- Fails to complete assigned tasks on time
- Does the job only halfway
- Attempts to justify poor performance with excuses or laying blame on others
- Is more concerned about what everyone else is doing (or getting) than what he or she is supposed to be doing (or getting)

I ponder the following questions: Is this normal for an eight-year old? Is it only a stage, or is he suffering from an attention deficit? If it's only a stage, is it gender specific, or will I have to prepare for the same behavior from his six-year-old sister when she turns eight? I also wonder whether a lack of consistency or effective communication on my part is exacerbating such problems. Could I be creating a future *bad employee*?

Even more worrisome: If my job is to be a good parent, and I am creating a bad employee, should *I* be fired?

Resurrection

One weekend we went out to buy a hamster for Michael. Jim and I had decided that it was time for Michael to have his own pet. Michael, of course, had been asking us for a pet since he was five, although the requested animal has changed from frog to turtle to hamster and back again many times. Michael had a hamster in his classroom, and Jim had had hamsters as a child, so it was a unanimous decision that his first pet should be a hamster.

Elizabeth was staying with us for the weekend, so the lot of us loaded ourselves into the car at 10:00 on

Saturday morning. I was certain we'd be home within an hour, mission satisfactorily accomplished. However, amid a selection of other rodents, the pet store had only one hamster, and it was brown. Jim offered a chance to look elsewhere so Michael could at least have choices.

The second store did not have any regular hamsters but carried a smaller breed known as "dwarf" hamsters. We were immediately helped by an amiable young woman who within seconds asked if we had considered a guinea pig.

"They're bigger, calmer, easier for the children to hold," she told us. "You can even walk them on a leash—see," she pointed at a display rack. "It's like a harness. And they can live up to eight years."

Michael stared at the display of harnesses with a look of glee on his face, and I, too, imagined how adorable it would be to walk down the street with a one-pound fur ball on the end of a leash. But the look of dismay on Jim's face reminded me of her last words; I was certain he was picturing Michael at the age of sixteen, begging to borrow the car keys while the long-abandoned guinea pig (harness piled on the floor next to the cage) remained in his room alone.

Jim immediately shook his head and told the woman we were set on a hamster.

She nodded and reached into a nearby cage, pulling out a dwarf hamster. As she tried to hand it to Michael, the tiny thing was so wild and fast that it nearly escaped from her hands, and she ended up putting it right back into the cage. "They're young; they take some time to socialize," she explained.

It was obvious that the dwarf hamster was too small and too fast for a small child to hold, so our search continued. We called two other stores to confirm that they had regular hamsters before we started our drive across town.

After a twenty-minute jaunt we entered store number three to find nothing but empty cages. I approached a young woman wearing a smock with the store logo. "We called. They said you had teddy-bear hamsters."

She walked to the cages with me, noted that they

were empty, and then stated unapologetically, "Looks like we sold out."

I turned to Jim; his frustration was more evident than mine. Back in the car I called a fourth store but this time asked them to check the cages. It was confirmed: they had a total of five hamsters! But today nothing would be easy. Instead of fifteen minutes to certain victory, we were stuck in a construction zone jammed with Saturday-afternoon traffic. Meanwhile, Elizabeth was complaining that the sun was coming in on her side of the car.

"I need something to drink!"

"We're almost there!" I tried to reassure her. "We'll get you something at the store."

Michael remained silent, probably worried that any complaining could jeopardize the mission.

Shortly thereafter the four of us stood in front of a row of cages labeled "Teddy Bear Hamsters." The holy grail of the day, they were filled with snuggling, furry creatures. As we all leaned closer to peer into the cages, a friendly young girl named Jessica approached, offering her help.

"We'd like to buy a hamster."

Jessica looked down at Michael and Elizabeth and, to our surprise, hesitated. Sorting through her key chain, she selected a key and stuck it into the lock of the hamster cage. She looked over at us and asked clearly, "You do know that hamsters bite, don't you?"

"Yeah, I had hamsters," said Jim. "I was bitten once or twice."

"I won't even pick them up by hand," she replied. "Have you considered a rat?" She stuck her hand into the cage and scooped one of the hamsters into a small plastic container—obviously so she would not be *bitten*. Jim reached out and took the hamster from her, holding it in his big, manly hands while the creature squirmed and wiggled to get away.

Then Jessica began to educate us on the subject of rats. She explained that comparing domesticated rats to wild rats was like comparing a dog to a wolf. Rats, we soon learned, are the smartest rodent of all (except perhaps for squirrels) and can even be taught to come when they are called. They can also be trained to do a variety of tricks and to play games such as hide-and-seek, and they can be litter trained. Soon the hamster was returned to its home and she was leading us to the rat cage. Reaching in with her bare hands, she pushed aside the pile of aspen shavings and picked up the lone gray baby rat.

"They don't bite," she reminded us and, gently tipping up the rat's nose, ran her finger across his little rat lips and teeth to prove that she was telling the truth. She handed the rat to Michael, not Jim. "They don't bite, and they're very social."

Soon we came to understand that the term "social," when used in regard to rats, had two meanings. First, they are very friendly to people and will bond with humans in a manner much like a canine. Second, they are not happy being isolated; it is best to have more than one rat.

Michael looked up at us with his big blue eyes, and

I realized that he had been extraordinarily patient throughout the day. "Can I *please* have a rat?" he begged, his hands cupped around the small gray critter, whose nose and whiskers poked out between his fingers. The little black eyes seemed to look right at me, waiting along with Michael for my answer.

Not wanting the newest family member to be lonely, I turned to Jim. "And one for Elizabeth, too?"

"Okay," he said.

You'd think that would have been the end of it, but remember, we'd driven fifteen miles to this store because it had plenty of *hamsters,* not rats. It seemed we were holding the only baby rat in the building. Jessica brought over a little carton and put the rat inside, handing it to Michael. We asked him to hold it carefully, and both children peeked through the tiny slats to make sure the rat was really in the box.

While Michael and Elizabeth wandered into the next aisle to pick out a rat house, we turned to Jessica. "Would you mind calling the store closest to our house? We were looking at hamsters there this morning, but we'd like to make sure they have baby rats before we drive all the way back toward home."

"Sure," she replied. "But make sure you get another male." She explained that a female rat can give birth to as many as twelve babies every twenty-five days. Unless we wanted our own breeding operation it was imperative that both rats be the same sex.

Five hours after having first left our house, we were back at the store where our day had started. The next rat would be Elizabeth's. Because Elizabeth was a six-year-old kindergartener obsessed with Barbies and Polly Pockets, whose favorite color was any shade of pink and who could list every single Disney princess in less than fifteen seconds, we (rightly or wrongly) lied to her by telling her she would be getting a girl rat. Jim pulled aside the employee about to help us pick out our second rat and asked if he would please refer to all of the males as "she."

Back in the car, each child quietly peered into his or her own carton. Then Elizabeth announced that she thought she saw a raisin in the bottom of her rat's box. Jim and I could barely contain our laughter.

The children spent the whole evening watching their rats. Elizabeth named hers Jasmine, after the Disney princess from *Aladdin,* and Michael named his George. Only Jim and I seemed to notice that Jasmine's testicles were bigger than George's.

The next morning we closed off the master bathroom and let the rats loose. While Michael and Elizabeth giggled, the rats ran under the cabinets and across the floor, climbed up the children's arms and down their backs, and jumped down again onto the travertine. From time to time, they would also leave a trail of . . . raisins.

All went well for the next three days. On the fourth Michael and I started our day to find Jasmine lying on his stomach with his head down and one leg hanging loosely through the metal grid of the second level of the cage.

"Jasmine?" I asked, as though he could answer me. "Are you feeling okay?"

Elizabeth had returned to her mother's house after our weekend together, so it was only Michael who stepped over to take a look in the cage. "Maybe she's just tired," he offered.

I reached in and took Jasmine out of the habitat; he lay unresponsive in my hand. I began to panic but tried to hide it from Michael. I set Jasmine down on the table, certain he would begin to wander, but instead he just flopped down and remained still.

"You should take her to the vet."

Instinctively I thought, "That's not going to help." But instead I said, "Maybe you're right, honey; maybe she's just tired. But if she doesn't seem better by the time I get home from work, I'll take her to the vet." I placed Jasmine gently in the bottom of the cage, knowing this wasn't going to turn out well. "C'mon, let's go to the bus."

Michael and I walked to the bus stop, and I tried to act normal. But once he was off to school I jogged back to the house and into the family room, where I peered into the cage to see that Jasmine's eyes were closed and his body perfectly still.

"Oh, no," I said out loud. "Oh, no!" I reached in to touch him, and his little body was stiff. I was already crying as I dialed Jim on the telephone.

"Hello."

"Jasmine is *dead*!"

"What?"

"He's dead!"

I explained the short series of events, still in disbelief.

"Can you pick him up? Put him in a shoebox or something?"

"No!"

"Well, you've got to get him out of the cage. Is George okay?"

"Yes, he seems fine!"

"Let me call you back," he said.

Jim was at work, Michael was on the bus halfway to school, and I was home alone with a dead rat. I needed to go to work, too, and there was nothing I could do for Jasmine. But I didn't want to leave George alone with a dead cagemate. Armed with a shoebox and a paper towel, I stuck my hand back into the cage. I covered Jasmine with the paper towel and then picked him up, closing my eyes even though I couldn't see him. His whole body was stiff, and I was shocked that rigor mortis had occurred so quickly. I put the tiny body into the box and took it to the laundry room. I washed my hands (for a long time), dried my eyes, and headed off to work, my cell phone ringing as I went. It was Jim.

"I put him in a box."

"You did?"

"Yeah. It was awful!"

"I'm sorry, honey."

His sympathy made me begin to cry all over again. "Honey, we need to get a replacement."

"What do you mean?"

"I mean a decoy. I'm all for kids learning about nature, but it's only been four days. I don't want them to worry every morning when they wake up that their new pet might be dead or dying. It would be different if we'd had them for a few months—even a few weeks—but not four days."

Jim never really said whether he agreed or not, but he promised to do as I asked. The pet store agreed to replace the rat, but they didn't have any with the same color pattern as Jasmine. Of course the solid-gray rat had survived, the one that would be easiest to replace without anyone knowing the difference. The one that had died had a white body and face and a black back. The closest Jim could get was a rat with similar coloring except with a black face instead of white.

When Jim brought Michael home from school, we avoided the cage or any discussion of the rats, not wanting to draw attention to them. It wasn't until long after dinner that Michael asked if we could take them out to play. All went well for the first ten minutes, and I actually believed we were in the clear.

But then he spoke: "Jasmine looks different."

I continued to play with George, avoiding eye contact with Michael. "Really?"

"Yeah. Her face used to be white."

"Really?"

"Yeah. I'm pretty sure it was white, and now it's black."

"Oh, I don't know; she looks the same to me."

Of course the moment Michael was in bed, I told Jim about his comments. "He didn't push the issue, so maybe he'll just let it drop." I also told him that I wanted to take the rats with us on our planned weekend trip in our motor home. "I'm not going to leave home and spend the weekend fearful we're coming home to a dead rat—or rats."

Two days later we loaded everything and everyone into the motor home and picked up Elizabeth at her mother's house on our way out of town. Elizabeth had already patted Max on the head and peeked under the sheet covering the rat cage to say hello to George and Jasmine. Now the children were tucked into their places with headphones and a DVD in play.

"I bet she won't even notice," I whispered to Jim. "After all, she was only around the rats for a day and a half before she had to return to her mother's house."

"It probably won't even come up," he said.

Four hours later we reached our destination and pulled into our camping spot. Jim stepped outside to set up the motor home while I removed the sheet from the rat cage and began to stock water and Gatorade in the refrigerator. Michael and Elizabeth were now peering into the cage, talking to the rats, and my heart stopped as they began to discuss Jasmine.

"Jasmine's face turned black!" Elizabeth said.

"I noticed that, too," replied Michael.

"That's weird. Did you see it happen?"

"No, it was that way one day when I got home from school."

I was frozen in place, trying to remain quietly in the background while still being able to eavesdrop on their conversation. It was all I could do to contain my laughter as I heard Michael continue, "You know, Oreo, the hamster in my classroom, she changed colors, too. She stayed in her little house for about three days, and when she finally came out, her back was gray, and she was fatter. And uglier, too."

"Really?"

"Yeah."

And then they stood and walked out of the motor home. I was laughing out loud. I was also feeling relieved to know that Michael's teacher was also guilty of the "switcheroo." I followed the children outside and immediately sought out Jim, who was visiting with our campmates. I told him about Elizabeth and Michael's conversation, and he, too, began to laugh. As our friends heard the story, through their laughter they shared a knowing glance with one another.

"Not you, too?" I asked.

"Oh, yes," they told us. "Goldfish—and parakeets. But luckily for us, no one ever noticed the differences."

Michael and Elizabeth didn't speak about Jasmine's color change for the rest of the weekend. In fact, they didn't bring it up again for a long while. And then one evening, months later, Jim came into our bedroom after a phone conversation with Elizabeth. He told me Elizabeth had asked him if Jasmine had changed colors lately. He'd told her no and, hoping the discussion would end quickly, attempted to change the subject. "What would you like to do this weekend?" he asked.

He was laughing so hard he could barely get the words out.

"Can we go back to the pet store?" she replied. "I want to watch the baby rats change colors."

EXCUSES

Michael is eight and in the second grade. I've watched him enter and depart many stages of development since he first came into my life. But lately things have been a little challenging, and I feel as though I have become the clichéd broken record: "Tie your shoes." "Turn off your lights." "Close your drawers." I have been saying these things to him since he entered school, yet he still fails to remember these simple tasks.

In first grade, even though I had to ask for the same things repeatedly, he would do what he was told to do.

Now, when queried, he provides a justification as to why it isn't done or an excuse why he cannot.

Tie your shoes.

> *I forgot.*
> *I did, but they keep coming undone.*
> *I need new laces, these are too hard to tie.*
> *I don't like these shoes; I need a new pair.*
> *I need to brush my teeth.*
> *Will you do it for me?*

Turn off your bedroom lights.

> *I forgot.*
> *I didn't know they were still on.*
> *It was dark, and I needed to see.*
> *I didn't have a chance to do it.*
> *I need to rinse out my cereal bowl.*
> *Will you do it for me?*

Close your dresser drawers.

> *I forgot.*

There are too many clothes in them.
I didn't know they were open.
I was putting my laundry in the basket.
Will you do it for me?

Put your dirty clothes in the basket.
I forgot.
I didn't know they were on the floor.
The basket is full.
I was closing my drawers.
Will you do it for me?

Rinse out your cereal bowl.
I forgot.
I didn't know it was still on the counter.
I was putting away the cereal box.
Will you do it for me?

I can report with absolute certainty that repeating the words "I've told you a thousand times; why can't you remember?" serves absolutely no purpose.

Who Is in Charge?

Jim and I agree that a child should learn to respect those in authority. This doesn't mean blind obedience, and we try to teach Michael the difference. But sometimes a child must do as he is told whether he wants to or not—pick up his toys, put away his dishes, brush his teeth—because there will be a time in his life when he has to do other, more important things that he doesn't feel like doing. It may be a school assignment or a job task or giving up fun to help a family member, but it is better to learn discipline when you are young than to have none and struggle as an adult. Defying conformity is a personal choice, but it comes with consequences. If you don't do your dishes, you may not get your allowance, but as an adult, if you refuse to perform your job as required, you may get fired—a far worse consequence.

Somehow we have attempted to teach Michael these lessons in part by using the phrase "in charge." When we were first dating and I offered to watch Michael when Jim worked late, Jim would tell Michael that while Daddy was gone, Kate was "in charge." Michael has always been instructed that, whether it be a babysitter, Grandma, or my sister, that person is "in charge." Those in charge are to make certain Michael goes to bed at the right time, finishes his dinner if he wants dessert, and changes the channel if *SpongeBob SquarePants* comes on.

Michael became six and then seven and at the age of eight he now knows who is in charge without being told. Like any child, he has found ways to apply this concept, circumvent it, and test how far it extends. For example, he has figured out that because Grandma is

Jim's mother, Grandma is "in charge" of Daddy. He has also learned that when Jim is gone and I am the one to stay with him, he can get more and get away with more. And if I say, "No, you know your dad wouldn't approve of that," he'll say, "But Kate, you're in charge right now." Sometimes when both Jim and I are home, Michael will pursue me alone with his demands, hoping to wear me down. And when I begin to lose my resolve, I say, "You'll have to ask Daddy; he's in charge right now." Michael always sighs when I tell him Daddy is in charge because Daddy does not argue or negotiate or explain or justify; he simply says either "Yes" or "No." There's not much fun in that, so Michael likes to find ways to make sure I'm the one in charge.

A few weeks ago, on Mother's Day, we planned to meet Grandma and Papa and spend the day at the zoo. Before we left the house Michael asked his usual question, directed of course, toward me: "Can I get a toy at the zoo?"

However, it was Jim who replied, "No."

Michael looked disappointed for a moment, then turned to me and smiled. "But Kate, today is Mother's Day—you are in charge!"

This morning Michael asked if I would be able to come to his open house at school next week. It is an opportunity for parents to see the projects the children have been working on all year long. I can usually sneak away from work for an hour, but I never know when something may come up that will require my immediate attention. In previous visits to similar school events, I have seen children sobbing uncontrollably because their parents were not in attendance. I don't want Michael to be hurt or upset if I can't make it, so I try to manage his expectations.

"I am going to try to come to the open house, but it is taking place during my workday, and I may not be able to get there if something important comes up."

Michael ponders this for a moment. "You mean something like work that you have to do for Gordon?"

"Yes."

He thinks about this a little bit more. "Kate, is Gordon in charge of you?"

I can see where this is going. "Yes."

"Well, then, why don't you just ask him?"

There's no arguing with that logic.

Michael Age Nine, Elizabeth Age Seven

Elizabeth asks me to play charades with her from a children's version of the game. She selects a card and acts out a word, and I guess it. Then she pulls another card out of the box. This time she wraps her arms around herself and turns from side to side, as a person would do when cold. As I look at her, I notice that Elizabeth is mouthing something at the same time. Over and over, she mouths what looks like the word "warm."

"Is the word 'warm'?" I ask.

She smiles and nods, as though I figured it out on my own.

I tell the children that I am going to take them shopping for Father's Day gifts. I say I will tell Daddy that we're

going shopping for household things, just the three of us, and that they must keep it a secret that we are really shopping for his present. Michael says to me, "Okay, but Kate, don't act suspicious!"

Later the same day Jim goes off to run errands on his own, and I take the children and all the gifts up to Elizabeth's room so we can wrap them. Michael closes the bedroom door "in case Daddy comes home." I realize I have left the tape downstairs, so I get up, go out the door, close it, then turn around and knock three times.

"Come in!" they call out together.

I poke my head in and say, "What if it was Daddy? You can't let anyone in! I'm going to make a secret knock so you'll know it's me!"

I make up a distinct knock and demonstrate it for them. Then I close the door and again, knock three times.

"Don't come in!" they yell loudly.

I open the door. "Good job," I say.

I close the door and this time I knock on it using the secret knock.

"Come in!" they call out.

A while later we are just about finished wrapping the gifts. I ask Michael to take the rolls of paper downstairs and put them away in the hall closet. He walks out and closes the door. Then we hear a knock on the door: three times. I look at Elizabeth, and she looks at me.

"Don't come in!" we yell.

Michael opens the door and peers in. "I was just testing you!"

Michael: "Kate, I made up a joke. Do you want to hear it?"

Me: "Sure."

Michael: "What does a knight watch on television?"

Me: "Hmmm, I don't know. What does a knight watch on television?"

Michael: "The Knightly News."

I am searching through the kitchen drawer, trying to find the scissors. I'm trying to recall who might have used them

last. It doesn't take me long to figure out where they might be.

Michael is going through a phase in which he is constantly building things with tape and cardboard. I march up to Michael's room and find the scissors on the floor among a pile of boxes, tape, string, construction paper, and empty toilet-paper and paper-towel tubes.

I take the scissors downstairs, where he is parked on the sofa, watching cartoons.

"Michael, I need to talk to you about the scissors you stoled."

"Kate," he replies, "is it okay if I tell you something?"

"Yes, what is it?"

" 'Stoled' isn't a word."

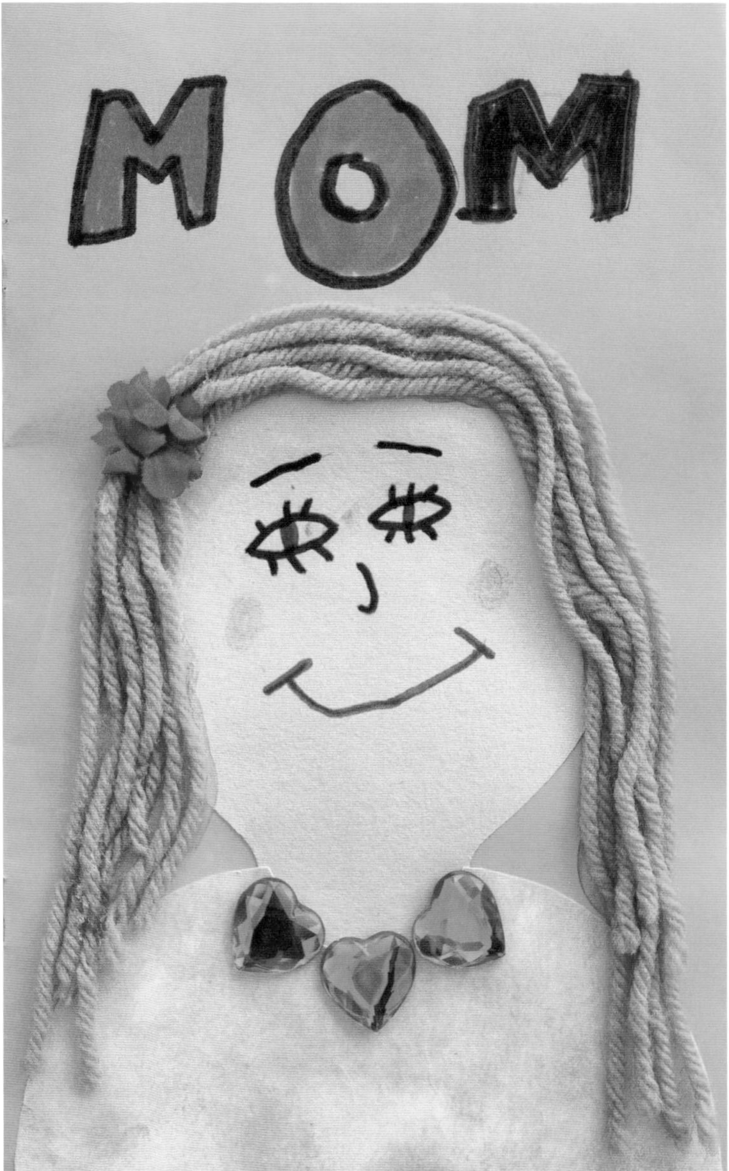
MOM

Breaking Up

Jim told Michael over the weekend that we are breaking up. We hadn't planned on telling him yet, but Michael had an inkling that something was going on and began to ask questions. When Jim confirmed that we were separating and they would be moving to a new house, Michael had many more questions. Jim told Michael that I would always be a part of his life, but Michael wanted to know more: Where exactly would they live? Where would he go to school? Would Elizabeth still get to see me? Jim answered the questions as best he could. When asked about moving, Jim told Michael he would still have his own room and that I had promised to buy him a set of new bunk beds. Jim told Michael that perhaps he and I could pick them out together.

I had been out of town for the weekend, and Jim called to tell me what had transpired when I was just moments from pulling into the driveway. We cried together on the phone as he described their discussion and advised me to be prepared for questions when I arrived. I had only a few minutes to pull myself together, but I walked into the house and immediately offered bear hugs and kisses, telling Michael how much I had missed him. But he did not ask me a single question about anything.

We all ate dinner together, and Michael and I did the dishes and put away the clean laundry. Then we sat side by side while I watched television and he played one of his electronic games. I asked him to take a bath while I got his backpack ready for the school week. I tucked him into bed. But he did not say one word about what he and his father had discussed.

The next day I thought Michael might question me on the way to the bus stop or while getting ready for school. But again he did not. After dinner we took out his homework and everything else he needed to do for the evening and spread it out on the counter. It wasn't until we were sorting through his Cub Scout book to determine what badges he had earned that he turned to me and said, "Kate, when are you going to buy my bunk beds?"

Stunned, I replied calmly that as he and Daddy were camping this weekend with the Cub Scouts, perhaps we could go together the following weekend.

Michael turned his head, covered his face with his hands, and began to cry.

I began to cry, too. I pulled him toward me and held him, and we cried together. When I could compose myself, I told him I loved him more than anything. I told him I would still see him all the time and talk to him whenever he wanted to. He pulled away and looked up at me with tears rolling down his freckled cheeks while I told him I would love him forever and that I will still love him when he was grown up and had children of his own.

His tears stopped falling but still rimmed his eyes.

"Some things will change, Michael, but a lot of things won't. I'll still tell you to turn off your bedroom lights and put your clothes in the basket. I'll still tell you to close your drawers, and you'll still have to help empty the dishwasher. We'll still go shopping at Target together, and you'll still ask me one hundred times if you can get something, and I'll still give in and buy it. We'll still go to the movies together, and we'll still go out to dinner. You'll still have to throw the ball for Max, and we'll still buy carrots for George and Jasmine."

A glimpse of a smile began to appear. But then it faded quickly. "Kate," he said, "it stinks that I have to change school districts."

I wanted to laugh, wondering where on earth he had picked up such an expression. But I reflected on just how perfect it really was. "You know what, honey? It does stink. But you know how sometimes we go camping, and other families show up who we haven't met before, and then you make new friends?"

"Yeah."

"Well, I'm sure that when you go to your new district, you'll make new friends, but then you'll still have your old friends over here, so you'll actually end up with twice as many friends. And now you'll have a bunk bed for your friends to stay in if you have a sleepover. So even though some things will change and there will be some things that you may not like, there will also be good things that will happen."

The tears were drying, and he nodded slightly.

"If you want, we can pick out some really cool sheets to go with your bunk beds."

"Okay."

Then silence, each of us waiting for the other to either continue or stop.

"You know how much I love you, right?"

A nod.

"More than anything in the whole world. And if

you have any more questions or want to talk about anything at all, you just let me know, okay?"

"Okay."

I waited for a while longer, but it seemed he had nothing more to say.

"Do you want to finish going through your Cub Scout book?"

Another nod.

Within minutes he was back to being a normal nine-year-old, as though our sad conversation and tears were a thing of the distant past.

When he turned his attention to his homework, I told him I had to go to the bathroom. I shut myself in and cried a thousand more tears, none of them doing anything to release the sadness I was feeling. How could life go on for me without Michael in it every day? And how would Michael deal with these changes?

Jim and I had both been previously divorced and were well schooled in surviving a separation. For us, I knew relief and hope would follow the grief and resentment that come with an ending. But I was sick with the stress of wondering what kind of chaos and sorrow would fall upon Michael, now being thrust into an unknown future.

How could we convince Michael that we would do our best to make everything okay, especially when his real mother had disappeared from his life when he was only two years old? Would this cause him to worry that I might disappear, too? Would he be forever damaged by the many changes in his short life and develop a never-ending fear of abandonment? Or could we, with love and understanding, help him to overcome the odds? Would he believe what I said or find any comfort in thinking that many aspects of his life would not change? Could I give him any peace at all by attempting to retain our rituals as best I could, even if most of them were small or silly?

When I tucked him into bed that night, he asked me, as he had nearly nightly in the last six years, what he should dream about.

"Tonight why don't you dream that you're on your camping trip . . . and that you get all of your Cub Scout badges and all of your arrows . . . and you have more badges than any other kid at camp?"

Lately my stories were too boring for him, and he would often ask for a second or third version. Tonight he simply replied, "Okay," and smiled.

I tucked the blankets up to his chin and kissed him again on the forehead.

"Kate?"

"Yeah, honey?"

"Are the rats going to go with us?"

"Yes, they're going to live with you, honey. They're your pets."

"Will you still get to see them?"

"Yes! I will come over and hold and kiss George whenever I can."

"Kate?"

"Yes?"

"When I leave, I'm going to call you every night and ask you what I should dream about."

A short while later, alone in the living room with my second round of tears in the works, I was still able to muster a smile. It seemed that my commitment to keeping as many things as I could the same, to preserving our many rituals, would not fall on my shoulders alone but would instead be a joint effort between me and the boy already asleep in the room upstairs.

The Best Thing That Ever Happened to Me

Now that Michael knows the relationship between me and his father is coming to an end, I am doing everything I possibly can to keep our lives seemingly normal. I want him to see that Jim and I can get along and that taking care of Michael will remain (as much as it can) a shared responsibility. I want him to know I am committed to preserving as many routines as I possibly can. More than anything, I want him to know and feel that he is loved.

This morning we are getting ready for school, about to head out to the bus stop. I turn to Michael and say,

"Honey, you do know that the issues between me and your dad have nothing to do with you? And do you know that we both love you very much?"

Michael smiles and nods. He has a look that says, "Don't worry; I've got it all figured out." But he is still only nine years old, and I can't believe that he does.

I put my arm around him, and we walk out the front door, down the sidewalk, and out into the street, heading toward the bus stop.

"Michael, do you know what the best thing to ever happen to me was—in my whole entire life?"

He looks into my eyes, saying nothing, and waits for me to answer.

"Being your mom."

Michael smiles. "I know."

LIES

How can you teach a child not to lie when you are a liar? I cannot ask Michael's father that question, but it is one I wish he would answer.

During the course of our breakup, Jim told me in person and in writing that he would never keep Michael from me. In the moments of trying to comfort Michael as his world began to change around him, I promised that I would always be there for him. Now his father is failing to keep his word and making every meeting a challenge.

Our breakup occurred in March, but for Michael's

sake we agreed they should continue to live with me through the end of the school year. After witnessing the never-ending conflict between Jim and Elizabeth's mother, I wanted to prove to Jim that a breakup could be managed kindly and cordially. Jim made an offer on a house with a closing date in mid-June and spent the last two months of our cohabitation asking me for help of every kind. I obliged nearly every time, desperate to remain on good terms. I convinced myself that whatever help I offered Jim would benefit Michael.

Sadly, I came home after a weekend away with a girlfriend to find that Jim had moved them out of the house ten days early without telling me he was going to do so. My last week with Michael had come and gone, and I hadn't even been aware of it.

To add to the insult, the house looked as if a robbery had taken place; there were stacks of boxes and belongings scattered about in nearly every room. Jim told me on the phone that most of what remained needed to be thrown out or taken to Goodwill. I quickly realized he had no intention of doing it himself. Along with room after room of things left behind that I now had to dispose of, Jim had also left George and Jasmine.

I was exasperated. "They are the children's pets!"

"Well, I don't have any room for them," he told me.

I was upset that he had moved out without notice, angry that he had left so much behind for me to clean up, and frustrated that I would now be responsible for the care and feeding of two young rats. I wanted to scream, I wanted to yell, I wanted to dump everything in the front yard of his new house.

But I had to focus my attention on the only thing that really mattered: time with Michael.

Shortly after they moved out, Jim allowed me a long weekend with Michael while he went back East for a high school reunion. Michael and I went shopping for books and went to the movies. He played his Gameboy while I did laundry. We watched movies at home and made hot dogs. Other than the absence of his father, in all aspects it felt like a normal weekend. I was thankful that I got to spend these days with Michael and hopeful that it would be the first of many weekends together.

When Jim returned from his reunion he took Michael and Elizabeth camping for seven days. The trip had been planned for months, originally as a family vacation, but now I was home alone, feeling lost. I called Jim to ask if I could say hello to the children. He did not answer his phone. I left messages two days in a row. He did not return my call until the third day. I told the children I was happy they were having fun camping. Then I hung up the phone and cried.

When they returned from their vacation, I asked if I could have Michael for the weekend, and Jim told me I could not; they had plans to go out of town. I asked if I could instead have a dinner during the week. He told me Michael's grandmother was watching him during his workdays until school started; if I wanted to see him I must go to the other side of town and pick him up at Grandma's house. I made the long drive to get Michael, and we went out for pizza and ice cream, then went to Target to shop for school supplies. Among other things, we picked out a backpack. It had wheels like a suitcase, and Michael rolled it around the store with a smile on his face. I tried to be cheerful, tried to act happy, but it all felt so artificial, so forced. I dropped Michael off at his grandmother's house and drove away in tears.

The next time I saw Michael, after his trip out of town and again just for a dinner, he told me his daddy didn't want him to have a backpack with wheels and had bought a different one for him. I was frustrated, but I told Michael it was okay, he could use the backpack with wheels for traveling instead of for school. Michael also told me a little about his trip, and although I wanted to ask questions, I did not. I had already figured out most of it.

I was fairly certain that during Jim's high school reunion, he had reunited with a former girlfriend, a woman with whom he had recently reconnected with on Facebook (while lying in bed next to me with his laptop computer and telling me she was just an old friend from high school). She lived in Las Vegas, and Jim traveled to see her every other weekend—with Michael in tow. I wondered how he could sleep in the same bed with this woman so quickly after leaving me and not worry what Michael would think. I wondered why he didn't let me care for Michael during those weekends until he had determined the seriousness of the relationship. But I had no right to question his behavior.

Over the course of three weeks I got only one week-night dinner with Michael. Michael revealed that Jim had told him he would have to leave for work before Michael needed to leave for school, so Michael would have to pack his own lunch and go to the bus stop alone. In the afternoons he would be required to get off the bus by himself and go home to an empty house to do his homework. I drove home that night sobbing.

I had offered to pay for Michael's before- and after-school care, I had offered to pay for Michael to eat lunch in the cafeteria. Jim told me neither thing was necessary. I didn't know Michael would have to pack his own lunches; I didn't know he would be relegated to latchkey child. I wondered why Jim didn't worry that a nine-year-old boy could be kidnapped on his way to the bus stop, or that something could happen to him at home while he was alone for hours at a time.

I sent Michael a funny greeting card by mail, telling him that I loved him and missed him. I told him on the phone that when I saw him next we would go to a new movie that had just come out. Days later I got an e-mail from Jim telling me not to tell Michael that I missed him because it was confusing for him. He said I should not promise Michael I would take him to a movie because Jim had told Michael he would take him. He revealed that he did not give Michael my greeting card because I didn't send one for Elizabeth.

I wanted to reply, "Of course it is confusing for

Michael!" I wanted to say, "You've never taken him to the movies!" I wanted to scream, "But Elizabeth has a mother. Michael does not!" Instead I said nothing, fearing any perceived infraction against Jim would result in missed time with Michael.

After all, I am not his birth mother; I am not his real mother. No matter how many snotty noses I cleaned, no matter how many scraped knees I bandaged, no matter how many times I held the bucket while he vomited—or did the million other things that mothers do—I have no rights.

As much as I struggled to see Michael, I also had to try to comprehend who this man was who stood in our way. He was someone I did not know, completely unlike the man with whom I had fallen in love. The man I loved bought romantic greeting cards for me and took his children shopping for Mother's Day gifts for me every year. The man I loved believed that the interests of the children should come first and told me I would always be in Michael's life.

I sorted through a box of mementos and found scores of notes and cards from Jim:

> *"Thanks for everything you've done for Michael and Elizabeth."*

> *"Thanks for taking care of Michael yesterday when he was sick."*

> *"I appreciate the understanding and care you give to Michael and Elizabeth."*

> *"It's so nice to know you've accepted Michael and Elizabeth (and obviously vice versa) and you treat them like your own."*

> *"Thanks for being such a great mother to Michael and Elizabeth."*

"Michael and I were getting dressed and we were talking about how wonderful you are to us."

I know that relationships change, and romantic love can fade. But how is it that all of my mothering, all of the efforts I made to be a good parent, all of the love I bestowed upon these two children now seems to have no value?

I read them over and over again, letters from a man who put into words his appreciation that I shared the responsibilities of raising his children, acknowledging that I loved them as my own and how much they loved me in return.

And I loved the man who wrote me these notes.

This new man was someone I did not recognize.

Another weekend came and went while Jim and Michael were in Las Vegas. The next time I saw Michael, he volunteered information about the new girlfriend's children. She had two boys who were ten and fourteen. Jim and the girlfriend had taken all three boys to the movies.

"That sounds like a good time," I told him. "I'm glad you're going on fun trips with your dad."

I didn't care that Jim had found another woman. But if she already had two boys of her own, how would she treat Michael? Would she be kind to him, or would he always be subjected to third place? I hoped and prayed that she was generous and loving.

By mid-August I was depressed and desperate for an escape. I planned a vacation to the beach with a girlfriend. Knowing I would be gone for nine days, I sent Jim an e-mail to ask if I could see Michael before I left. He told me I had to have him home by 8:30—school had started, and Michael had to go to bed early.

Michael and I went to Red Lobster, one of his favorite restaurants, for dinner. I tried to show an interest in his activities without appearing too nosy. I asked if he had made any new friends at school, and he told me yes, a little boy who wore glasses just like Michael and had also read all the Harry Potter books. As I inquired about Michael's new life, I had no way of knowing it would be the last time I would see him. But perhaps some part of my subconscious mind suspected it.

"Michael, do you know how much I love you?"

"Yes."

"Do you know that I wish I could see you all the time?"

"Yes."

"Do you know that I think of you every minute of every day?"

"Yes."

"Sometimes I ask to see you, and I can't because you and your daddy have plans. But I want you to know that I am always asking to see you, even if I'm not seeing you."

"I know."

"And sometimes I call you, but you and Daddy are busy, or on a trip, and I just have to leave a message.

But I want you to know that I always want to talk to you."

"I know."

"And you know that I will love you forever?"

"Yes. I know."

We left the restaurant and drove to Target. We picked out some books for Michael and Elizabeth, and Michael asked if he could sit down in the bottom of the shopping cart. He was nine, far too old to sit in a shopping cart. But on this night I would deny him nothing. He climbed into the back of the cart and nestled down among everything else, opened up one of his new books, and began to read. I pushed him around the store, pretending to shop.

"I love you, Michael," I said to him.

"I love you, too," he replied.

The Friday before my vacation I called and left a message for Jim, asking if I could speak to both Michael and Elizabeth before I went out of town. Jim did not return the call. I tried again in the morning before I left the house, but he did not answer. During my trip I left another message on Sunday and yet another on Monday. Wednesday evening my girlfriend and I came out of a loud restaurant and I found that I had missed a call from Michael. His message told me that he missed me and loved me. I called back but got no answer. I spent the entire evening and the following day of my vacation in tears.

Back home from my trip, I immediately telephoned Jim, but as was his way, he did not answer. I left a message, but he did not call me back. I e-mailed him, and he did not reply. All of my messages were the same: "When can I see Michael?"

The next day my world fell to pieces. I received an e-mail from Jim stating that he believed it was "in Michael's best interest" that we no longer have contact. I screamed, I yelled, I sobbed. He claimed that our family counselor had advised him on this issue, but I didn't believe a word of it: I had been seeing the family counselor all along, and he had told me the exact opposite.

I was in disbelief; I was in shock. I was devastated.

I cried for an entire week.

THE LAST WORD

The last time I spoke to Jim was by telephone. It had been more than a month since I'd last had contact with him. Upon the advice of our family counselor, I had sent Jim an e-mail asking if he would reconsider allowing me to see Michael. He telephoned me a few days later. I told him our counselor had said that even though the amount of time I spent with Michael would naturally lessen over time as our lives moved in different directions, he thought it best that I retain contact with him now, even if it was only in limited amounts. Jim insisted that the counselor had told him the opposite, but he did not provide any details or further insight into why.

For just a moment I wondered if the counselor was playing both sides for his own benefit. "If our counselor is telling you one thing and me another, why don't we go see him together?" I suggested.

Any doubts I had about the counselor's intentions were immediately cleared up by Jim's reply. "No, I'm not doing that," he said. "And besides, it's not going to change my mind."

"What have you told Michael about all of this?" I asked.

"I told him that people move on. You've moved on; we've moved on. People move on. You just need to let this go. I'm not changing my mind."

"I'll never let it go!" I screamed into the phone, and then I hung up on him. Although I can't recall specifically, it's also possible I called him an asshole.

But the fact remained that my threat carried absolutely no weight; there wasn't a thing I could do about any of this.

LIFE PATHS

I feel as though there has been a death. And there has been. The death of motherhood, the death of my child. I have been told I cannot see this boy, a child I raised for six years, yet my mind tells me he is only a fifteen-minute drive away. How can this be? What kind of logic is this? What have I done to deserve such punishment? I wonder how I will survive this loss. But more importantly, I wonder how Michael will survive it.

I was not so naive as to think I would get regular visitations, scheduled time, annual vacations, or invitations to every school event. But I thought I could remain a part of Michael's life as just one of many people who loved and cared about him. I was a big part of Michael's childhood and hoped I could remain a presence—even if just in the background—through his teens and into adulthood so he would know that even if people come and go, love does not have to. Sadly, that will not be the case.

My heart aches when I think that Michael, abandoned by his real mother, might believe I abandoned him, too. I am an adult; I can survive the pain and at least try to understand the psychology behind his father's actions. But Michael has just turned ten; no matter what his father has told him about my absence (of which I'll never really be certain), how can he understand any of it?

I continue seeing the family counselor, and I try to learn to deal with my loss. I am told that Michael's life path is his alone, and I am not responsible for it. I love that child with my full heart, but it is true that I have no control over Michael's journey and am not responsible for his father's actions. Still, it is impossible to

accept that Michael and I have to be dead to one another, gone from each other's lives, when I know all
the while that he is just across town.

And what of Elizabeth? I first met her at the age of
one, and nearly her whole life has included me. Does
she wonder why I've gone? Does she miss me? I cared
for Elizabeth alongside Michael whenever she came
to stay with us. I loved her, too. She would often crawl
into my lap on the sofa and tell me she loved me in
return. So much of my time with Michael was com-
mingled with caring for Elizabeth.

But Elizabeth has a mother, and Michael does
not. Knowing I cannot be there for him is like a knife
through my heart. I worry about him being alone, and
I cry for all the things I can no longer do with him: I
will not be able to have conversations with him, listen
to his observations, or answer any of his inquiries. I
cannot take him to the movies or shopping, or buy
Christmas and birthday gifts for him. No longer will
we squeeze into the reading chair together with our
books and our blanket. I will not be able to snuggle

him, laugh with him, make ketchup smiley faces on his plate, talk to him on the phone, or tell him every single day how very much I love him. I won't be there to see him change, grow, and develop.

I miss everything about him. I miss his freckles, his big blue eyes, his smile, his habits, his questions, his ideas, his creativity, his kindness, his sweetness—and it is like torture to me. I won't see his school projects. I won't be there the day he outgrows his stuffed animals. I won't get to meet his friends, be introduced to his first girlfriend, witness him getting his driver's license, or help him off to college.

For six years Jim asked me to help parent his son, and I did so. For six years I saw Michael nearly every single day, and now I have been told I cannot see him at all. For six years Jim stated that the interests of the children came first, and I believed him.

But here's the thing: even now, knowing the outcome, it is impossible to imagine changing any of the past because I cannot fathom giving up even one minute of those six years with Michael.

LETTERS

As the weeks roll by and I try to figure out how to live a life without Michael, two things strike me: first, how much I miss his companionship, and second, how much free time I have. Nearly half of my adult years were lived as a single person, and I have always had an active life. But now I have no idea what I did before I became a mother; I cannot remember how I filled my days when I lived alone.

Fortunately, I have amazing, generous friends and a dear, precious sister. These loved ones invite me to dinner, take me out, call me, let me talk about it, and let me not talk about it. Still, there are only so many dinners in a week, and the days are long and lonely. I wonder what Michael is doing, if fourth grade is difficult for him, if he is making new friends, if he is happy. I worry about him, too. Is he scared when he walks to the bus stop, nervous about coming home to an empty house? Does his father help him with his homework, or does he have to do it alone? Most of all I worry incessantly that he believes I intentionally abandoned him. I want to write to him, tell him I have not abandoned him, tell him again and again how much I love him. Although I know his father will not give him my letters, I decide that will not stop me from writing them.

And so my journal of letters to Michael begins. I write to Michael and tell him that I miss him, I love him, and I think about him every day.

The weeks turn into months, and I know I must find a way to live again. I decide to return to the sand dunes, a place where we always camped as a family. I arrive as a single person and take on the challenges of my sand rail and the motor home alone. It is difficult, but I push through my fears and insecurities and come home feeling capable and successful for handling everything on my own. It feels strange and different to be doing this without Jim, Michael, and Elizabeth. But it also helps me a little to be doing something I enjoy. I come home and write in the journal, telling Michael how often I thought of him while I was there.

On another weekend I go out to see my musician friends. They play in a band at a local night spot. They call me up on stage and let me sing a song with them. Everyone claps. I thank the band; I enjoy myself and go home to my dog. I write in the journal and tell Michael I miss him and recall a year ago when we went to see these same friends and Michael played the tambourine with the band.

At home in front of the television, the programming is interrupted by commercials for the latest Disney movie, and I am sad to know that I cannot talk to Michael about it, ask him if he wants to see it, make plans with him to do so over the weekend. I write again to Michael and tell him how I would love to take him to the movies, wondering how many he has seen without me.

Throughout all of this, I realize I am not only lost and sad but flabby and fifteen pounds overweight. At the advice of a friend, I join a gym and hire a trainer. As the pounds start to come off, so does my sadness. But missing Michael never goes away. I write and tell him so.

Another season of *American Idol* comes and goes, and I watch it faithfully, the spot on the sofa next to me terribly empty. I wish I could call Michael, ask him whom he is rooting for and who he thinks will get voted off next. But I can't. So I write to him and tell him how much I wish we were watching it together.

It is difficult for me to live a life without Michael, but now I have a way to tell him when I am thinking of him, a way to wish him a happy birthday or a merry Christmas or to remind him that the first time I ever met him was on a Mother's Day. I know the letters are as much for me as they are for him, but I write them in the hope that someday he will actually read them.

This past Easter I was especially frustrated by the fact that I could not buy Michael an Easter basket. For the prior six years I was the one who shopped for baskets and toys and Easter candy and helped the children to color Easter eggs, sometimes dragging along all the supplies to do so in the motor home. I wanted so badly to buy him a basket, wanted so much to be able to give him a gift. I opened a separate savings account that week and deposited five hundred dollars into it: one hundred for Easter and two to make up for Christmas and his birthday. The rest was for the days I could not buy him new Pokémon cards, new books to read, new clothes to wear, or a new game for his Gameboy. I wrote to him again and explained that I now had a way to give him presents for every holiday and that someday he could use the money to buy a car, or to go to college, or to do whatever he wants with it.

I put another hundred dollars into the account just before Mother's Day. As I write to Michael to say that being his mother was the best thing that ever happened to me, I realize it's been more than a year since Jim told me they were leaving, almost a year since they actually left. On Mother's Day I sort through the box of mementos from Michael and Elizabeth, including Mother's Day cards and dozens of school projects made just for me and addressed to "Mom." As I expected, I shed quite a few tears that day.

I realize I am finding ways to live a life without Michael in it, but I never stop thinking about him, and I never stop missing him. I have lost the fifteen pounds, I have changed my hairstyle. I have purchased new clothes and wear high heels more often. I make a trip with friends to the annual motorcycle rally in Laughlin, Nevada, something I've done (with and without Jim) for the past ten years. I drink and dance and gamble and welcome flirtations from attractive men. I return home and begin to accept invitations to date, but I know I am ready for no more than an occasional dinner companion. When I come across a man with young children, I am torn between wanting to run away from all the potential complications and heartache and wanting to cleave to them just to be around a small person again. It feels strange to be dating; it feels odd to be kissed good-night. I wonder how it was that Jim could—and would—find someone almost instantly when a year after our breakup, I am overwhelmed by the prospect of more than one dinner invitation in the same week.

But I am living my life, and I am living it without Michael—what other choice do I have? In the meantime, I write my letters.

And I continue to hope with all hope that someday I will see him again.

*Thanks to Fred and Claudia for their
invaluable guidance on the manuscript.*

*Thanks to Candida, who has always encouraged
and inspired me to write—and keep writing.*

*And thanks to Gordon—for a million things—but
most of all for the time, space and place to write.
And the constant badgering.*